LETTERS
to My SON

LETTERS
to My SON

A Father's Wisdom on
Manhood, Life, and Love

Kent Nerburn
Foreword by Richard Carlson

NEW WORLD LIBRARY
NOVATO, CALIFORNIA

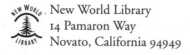 New World Library
14 Pamaron Way
Novato, California 94949

Cover design: Jason Gardner and Mary Ann Casler
Cover photo of Kent Nerburn and his father, Lloyd:
    Virginia Nerburn, 1948
Text design: Jason Gardner

Library of Congress Cataloging-in-Publication Data
Nerburn, Kent, 1946–
    Letters to my son : a father's wisdom on manhood, life, and love
/ Kent Nerburn ; foreword by Richard Carlson. — Rev. ed.
        p.   cm.
    ISBN 1-57731-031-4 (alk. paper)
    1. Young men—Conduct of life. I. Title.
    BJ1671.N48   1999
    170'.81—dc21   98-51499
                                                                  CIP

First printing, February 1999
ISBN 1-57731-031-4
Printed in Canada on acid-free, recycled paper
Distributed to the trade by Publishers Group West
10 9 8 7 6 5 4 3 2 1

For Nick, of course,
and every father's son

"We are born male.
We must learn to be men."

CONTENTS

Foreword by Richard Carlson xi

Introduction xiii

Prologue: A Father's Wish xvii

  1. The Shadow of the Father 1

  2. Man and Male 7

  3. Strength 13

  4. Rainaldi's Lesson 23

  5. Education and Learning 27

  6. Work 31

  7. Possessions 39

  8. The Miracle of Giving 47

  9. Money and Wealth 53

 10. Drugs and Alcohol 67

 11. Tragedy and Suffering 75

 12. Fighting 79

 13. War 83

 14. The Spiritual Journey 89

15. Loneliness and Solitude 97

16. Sports and Competition 103

17. Travel 107

18. The Blue Moment 117

19. Craig's Lesson 121

20. The Power of Art 129

21. Women and Men 133

22. Falling in Love 139

23. The Mystery of Sex 143

24. Making Love 149

25. The Haunted Heart 157

26. Partners and Marriage 161

27. Staying Faithful 167

28. Fatherhood 171

29. The Burden of Age 175

30. The Gift of Age 179

31. Death 183

Epilogue: A Father's Reflection 187

FOREWORD

WE ALL NEED ADVICE growing up and facing *the big stuff* life gives us. We all need the voice of a parent or a good friend who has lived through joy and suffering and has thought deeply about it. Kent Nerburn is an extraordinary writer who can be that voice when we are lost and in need of guidance. *Letters to My Son* — written for his son, Nick, but true for all of us — shows us that life isn't always easy or fun but that it is always a gift to be treasured and shared in all its richness with those we meet along the way.

We live in a time when no one wants to take the responsibility to say what's right and what's wrong — when no one wants to be told what to believe. Kent is that rare individual who's not afraid to be vulnerable, to stand up and speak from the heart. He shares with us what he believes, and makes us look at the hard questions, but never offers easy answers. Like a wise and gentle friend, he guides us to the truths that emerge when you approach life openly and honestly.

Letters to My Son gives us Kent's wisdom and experience, in beautiful, moving writing that speaks with amazing clarity and directness to the most important issues — *the big stuff!* — we all face in trying to live life happily, compassionately, and wisely. May you hear, enjoy, and prosper!

— Richard Carlson
Author of *Don't Sweat the Small Stuff…* and
Don't Sweat the Small Stuff with Your Family

INTRODUCTION

THIS IS NOT A BOOK I INTENDED TO WRITE. The world is full enough of grand moralizing and private visions. The last thing I ever intended was to risk adding my name to the long list of those involved in such endeavors.

Then, in midlife, everything changed. I was surprised with the birth of a son.

Suddenly, issues that I had wrestled with in the course of my life and questions that I had long since put to rest rose up again in the eyes of my child. I saw before me a person who would have to make his way through the tangle of life by such lights as he could find. It was, and is, incumbent upon me to guide him.

For now this is easy. His life does not extend much beyond his reach. I can take him by the hand and lead him. But before long he will have to set out on his own. Where, then, will he find the hands to guide him?

I look around and I am concerned. The world is a cacophony of contrary visions, viewpoints, and recriminations. Yeats's ominous warning that the best lack all conviction while the worst are filled with passionate intensity seems to have come to pass. Good men everywhere realize that the world we have made is also the world we have failed, that our brightest dreams and our greatest fears lurk just over the horizon. Acutely aware of both, we stand mute, driven by our hopes, silenced by our doubts.

I can no longer afford this silence. I want my son to be a man of good heart who reaches out to the world around him with an open mind and a gentle touch. I want him to be a man of belief, but not a man of judgment. I want him to have explored his own moral landscape so that he will not unwittingly do harm to himself or others. To be such a man he needs to hear voices that speak with empathy, compassion, and realism about the issues of becoming a man.

And so I take my place among those attempting to provide such a voice.

I bring to the task such skills as I have: a love of the language; a belief in the higher visions of the human species; a complex mélange of anger, wonder, and despair at the world in which we live; years of learning, miles of travel, a love for the wisdom of all spiritual traditions, and a faith in the inexhaustible miracle of the experience of life all around us.

But above all, I bring this:

One day last week a former student of mine methodically drove his car to the end of a street, pushed the accelerator to the floor, and catapulted himself off a cliff into a lake far below. On the same day I listened to a man speaking about his journey to India to study with a woman who could read his spirit by laying her hands on the sides of his head and staring into his eyes. That evening I found myself sitting with an old drunken man on a bench outside a store talking about the pleasures of catfish.

It is my gift to be able to embrace all these people and all their truths without placing one above the other. I can enter into their beliefs and give assent to each of them and learn from each of them. And I can pass their truths along.

This may not seem like much. But I value it above all else. The lonely old neighbor with her thirty-six cats, the shining young man at the door with his handful of religious literature, the good teacher, the honest preacher, the junkie, the mother, the bum in the park who told me never to take a job where I had to wear the top button of my collar buttoned and not to mess up my life like he did — I can hear all their truths and I can celebrate them.

If I can take these simple truths and elevate them beyond the anecdotal, I can offer something of value to my son and to other fathers' sons. I can offer a vision of manhood that is both aware of our human condition and alive to our human potential. I can offer the distilled insights of the dreamers and the doubters, the common and the rare. And in the process, perhaps I can reveal something about manhood to those readers, both male and female, who seek a compassionate place from which to survey the vast and confusing landscape before us.

— Kent Nerburn
Bemidji, Minnesota 1999

A Father's Wish

I WRITE THIS BOOK AS A FATHER — not just as your father but as any father. Until you have a son of you own, you will never know what that means. You will never know the joy beyond joy, the love beyond feeling that resonates in the heart of a father as he looks upon his son. You will never know the sense of honor that makes a man want to be more than he is and to pass something good and hopeful into the hands of his son. And you will never know the heartbreak of the fathers who are haunted by the personal demons that keep them from being the men they want their sons to see.

You will see only the man that stands before you, or who has left your life, who exerts a power over you, for good or for ill, that will never let go.

It is a great privilege and a great burden to be that man. There is something that must be passed from father to son, or it is never passed as clearly. It is a sense of manhood, of self-worth, of responsibility to the world around us.

And yet, how to put it in words? We live in a time when it is hard to speak from the heart. Our lives are smothered by a thousand trivialities and the poetry of our spirits is silenced by the thoughts and cares of daily affairs. The song that lives in our hearts, the song that we have waited to share, the song of being a man, is silent. We find ourselves full of advice but devoid of belief.

And so, I want to speak to you honestly. I do not have answers. But I do understand the questions. I see you struggling and discovering and striving upward, and I see myself reflected in your eyes and in your days. In some deep and fundamental way, I have been there, and I want to share.

I, too, have learned to walk, to run, to fall. I have had a first love. I have known fear and anger and sadness. My heart has been broken and I have known moments when the hand of God seemed to be on my shoulder. I have wept tears of sorrow and tears of joy.

There have been times of darkness when I thought I would never again see light, and there have been times when I wanted to dance and sing and hug every person I met.

I have felt myself emptied into the mystery of the universe, and I have had moments when the smallest slight threw me into a rage.

I have carried others when I barely had the strength to walk myself, and I have left others standing by the side of the road with their hands outstretched for help.

Sometimes I feel I have done more than anyone can ask; other times I feel I am a charlatan and a failure. I carry within me the spark of greatness and the darkness of heartless crimes.

In short, I am a man, as are you.

Although you will walk your own earth and move through your own time, the same sun will rise on you that rose on me, and the same seasons will course across your life as moved across mine. We will always be different, but we will always be the same.

And that is what this book is about. It is my attempt to give you the lessons of my life, so that you can use them in yours. They are not meant to make you into me. It is my greatest joy to watch you become yourself. But time reveals truths, and these truths are greater than either of us. If I can give them voice in a way that allows me to walk beside you during your days, then I will have done well.

To be your father is the greatest honor I have ever received. It allowed me to touch mystery for a moment, and to see my love made flesh. If I could have but one wish, it would be for you to pass that love along. After all, there is not much more to life than that.

LETTERS
to My SON

CHAPTER I

The Shadow of the Father

THE IMAGE OF MY FATHER floats like a spectre before me as I try to form my thoughts about manhood. I see him as he is now — a shell of a man, lost in private memories, spending his days idly flicking a television from channel to channel in hopes of finding something to occupy his time.

I see him as he is, but I remember him as he was.

I remember his strong back as he worked late into the night, weeding or raking or painting, the sweat forming a great, swooping arc down the middle of his spine.

I remember his perfectly ordered workbench in the basement with a hook for each tool and a label on every box.

I remember his outbursts of anger, his halting attempts to talk to me about sex.

I remember his silences and his diligence, his inarticulate efforts to show me through ritual what he could not say in words.

And I remember his unspoken pride as his children grew, graduated, found mates, and went off into life.

He remembers little of this. His memory has begun to

fail. The man who would recite me Lincoln's Gettysburg Address from memory can no longer remember the day of the week. His workbench is in shambles and bits of long-forgotten projects sit in dusty piles behind boxes in the corner. The man who in memory towered over me, all shoulders and biceps and strength, seems shriveled and small, cautious in his gestures and tentative in his gait.

I should feel sadness for this, and I do. But it is a sadness mixed with awe. With each passing day I realize more how much he lives within me, and how great a shadow he casts over my life.

It is the same for all men. None of us can escape this shadow of the father, even if that shadow fills us with fear, even if it has no name or face. To be worthy of that man, to prove something to that man, to exorcise the memory of that man from every corner of our life — however it affects us, the shadow of that man cannot be denied.

I am lucky. Though his anger ran deep and his heart was lonely at its core, my father did me no damage. His hand was always on my shoulder when I needed it, and he worked hard not to visit the sins of his father onto the life of his son.

Other men have not been so lucky. Their memories are filled with violence and brutality, the smell of alcohol, moments spent cowering in corners beneath the sound of breaking glass.

Others have only the aching emptiness where the memory of the father ought to be.

But we all labor under the shadow. It makes us who we are and shapes the man we hope to be.

To become a father is to understand the power of that shadow from the other side. You realize that the touches you make upon your son will shape him, for better or for worse, for his entire life.

And who can know which touches have meaning? A word here, a glance there, a time together, a time apart — which will be the moments that will rise up in memory and shape the child who looks without judgment on all that you do and say?

I see an image before me. It is an apartment hallway, bathed in half-light. My father stands there. I am behind him, a frightened ten-year-old, peering tentatively toward a door. We have a bicycle with us. It is a purple "racer," as we called them, with hand brakes and a gear shift. It is the most beautiful bike I have ever seen. We are returning it to its owner.

My father had found this bike on one of his early morning walks along a city beach. He had kept it in our garage, covered with a blanket. He wouldn't let me ride it because, he said, it belonged to someone else. For weeks that bike had stood in our garage as my father advertised in the local papers for its owner. I had secretly dreamed that the owner would never call so I could have that bike for my own.

But the owner did call, and now we are standing at his door prepared to return his bike to him.

My father knocks. The door opens a crack. A man peers out and looks past us both toward the bike. He pulls it in the door and examines it. My father and I stand in the doorway, waiting.

"It has a lot of new scratches on it," the man says.

My father says nothing.

The man turns the wheels, test the handlebars. He looks at my father accusingly. I want to cry out that there are no new scratches, that it has been under a blanket in our garage. Instead, I look down. The bike glints and shines in the hall-way gloom.

The man pulls it further inside and mutters, "I suppose I should give you something." He pulls out a crumpled bill and tosses it toward my father. My father gives it back.

The man glares at us and goes back to examining the bike.

We turn and walk down the hall. I grab my father's shirt. "Why were you so nice to that man?" I ask. "He was really mean."

My father keeps walking. "Maybe he'll pass it along some day," he says. I trail behind him through the spare yellow light. We never mention that bike again.

This image fades, recedes, is replaced by another.

It is many years later. I am visiting a local jail on some minor administrative task.

While I sit in the waiting room I notice the name of one of my former students on the prisoners' list. He has been arrested for some act of public drunkenness and destruction of property. It is not his first arrest.

I have always liked this boy. He has a winning smile and there is a genuine kindness and love of life somewhere deep behind his eyes. He has no family. He has spent his life being shunted from foster home to halfway house. He doesn't know who his father is and he claims he doesn't care.

I ask the jailer if I can see him.

The jailer escorts me through a series of steel doors, each one echoing a little hollower as it slams behind me. I am brought to an empty cement room that is bright with the lifeless glare of fluorescent light.

"Wait here," the jailer says.

He brings my student into the room. "Hi, Chris," I say. Chris doesn't answer. His eyes are scared and blinking. "He's been a little wild," the guard says, "so he's been in solitary. It will take him a while to adjust to the light."

Chris looks at me. His lip is quivering. "Please don't let them put me back in there," he says. His eyes are those of a frightened child.

"Please," he says again. I have never before heard him say please to anybody.

I look at him for a minute. All I can see are his frightened eyes.

"Okay," I say. "I'll do it." His lip quivers once and he breaks into a grin.

I contact the guards and pay Chris's bail. They bring him his clothes. I sign a few papers and take him out to my car. I buy him a hamburger, then drive him out to a house where he says he can stay. By the time we get there he is chattering away, full of his old bluster and swagger.

As I pull to a stop he jumps out of the car. "See ya," he says. He never even turns around.

The next day I am telling a friend about Chris. He gets angry and begins to lecture me. "I can't believe you did that," he says. "You let him hustle you, just like he hustles everybody. You should have let him rot in that jail. Maybe he would have learned that he can't talk his way out of everything. Why did you do such a stupid thing, anyway?"

I look down. "Maybe he'll pass it along some day," I answer.

My friend shakes his head and goes back to his work.

Somewhere, many miles away, my father stares blankly at a television screen.

CHAPTER 2

Man and Male

MY FATHER WAS NOT AN EXTRAORDINARY MAN. There could be no epics written about his accomplishments. But he was a good man. He never harmed another person willingly, and he was always ready to do a kindness for those in need.

For the last ten years I have watched him slowly lose interest in life.

He is not unhappy. He is beyond unhappiness. He is depleted and defeated by the losses that have taken all sense of self-worth from him. First it was his job, then his physical strength, and finally any sense of usefulness that gave him a way to value his presence on earth.

It is a sad thing to see. All of us still love him and respect him and honor him as the father, but he no longer loves and honors and respects himself. His world and his body have betrayed him.

How did such a thing happen? How could a man who was always strong suddenly become so weak? Why did he give up when the horizons of life still stretched out to unknown distances before him?

I am afraid he gave up because he no longer considered himself a man.

He had done his best to meet the image of the man he had been told he should become — to raise the brightest, be the strongest, earn the most, need the least. And he had done well. Perhaps not as well as he would have dreamed, but for a boy who was alone in the world by age sixteen, he was more successful than he might have hoped. He raised himself up, found a place in the world, and built a family with honor, dignity, and caring. What took place in his mind that caused him to value his achievements so little? Why should he, who started with nothing and accomplished so much, feel that his manhood is gone?

The answer is harsh but clear. He confused being a male with being a man.

Being a male is part of our biological coding. It has to do with strength, domination, territoriality, competition, and a host of other traits that were essential in the days when dominance was the key to human survival.

Being a man is something different. It is taking these male traits and forming them into a life that meets the demands of the world around you while serving the needs of others. It is action in service of a dream. It is being grounded in belief while reaching for the stars.

The world into which my father was born did not allow him to see his manhood as separate from his maleness. Mere survival called forth all the powers of aggression, competition, and physical strength he had to offer.

He was born into poverty. His father ran off. His mother died. Before he was even an adult he was swallowed up into the Great Depression. To get food he had to work and to get work he had to be stronger and work harder. Soon Nazism and Fascism appeared on the world stage, and he was called to take up weapons against other men. After the war was over, he came back with nothing and had to carve out a place for his family in an economic and social order he had never seen.

From his earliest childhood he had been cut adrift in a world where a person needed to emerge the winner to keep from being annihilated. No wonder his sense of manhood was so deeply tied to his sense of male dominance and mastery.

Now, as his body fails him, that sense of dominance and mastery has been replaced by a sense of dependence. He feels purposeless and meaningless. The loss of his job, the loss of his physical strength and sexual powers, the loss of his ability to control the world around him are the loss of his manhood. He is a shell, living out his days in a benign hopelessness.

It did not have to be this way. As his son, I see his real manhood. I see the man who went for days without sleep to help people who had lost their homes to fires and floods. I see the man who worked two, sometimes three, jobs to give his children Christmas presents and who always put his own needs last. I see a man who took his male strengths and put them in service of a vision of caring and sharing, and nothing can diminish his manhood in my eyes.

He was a good man. In a small way, he was a great man. But he cannot see this. He lived in a time when manhood meant maleness, and he measured himself by those terms.

But now the times have changed.

You were born into a different world that will present you with different gifts and challenges. A new vision of manhood will be called for that does not tie so closely into the more aggressive and competitive residues of our male character. You will need to search out new ways of expressing strength, showing mastery, and exhibiting courage — ways that do not depend upon confronting the world before you as an adversary.

To a great extent, you will have to find the ways for yourself. In times past there were rituals of passage that conducted a boy into manhood, where other men passed along the wisdom and responsibilities that needed to be shared. But today we have no rituals. We are not conducted into manhood; we simply find ourselves there.

When our bodies tell us we have arrived, it is with a desire and a longing and a sense of unfulfilled outreach. But what we think is manhood is nothing more than our maleness coming into full flower. And when maleness operates untempered with moral value, it visits damage upon the earth.

I want you to consider this distinction as you go forward in life. Being male is not enough; being a man is a right to be earned and an honor to be cherished. I cannot tell you how to earn that right or deserve that honor. But I can tell you that the formation of your manhood must be a conscious act governed by the highest vision of the man you want to be.

As you reach for that vision, the echoes of the male will

always be with you. The competitive, the dominating, the great sexual urgency and desire for outreach will always whisper. But if you are able to transform them, these male attributes will become the true measures of manhood — strength and honor and moral force; courage, sacrifice, and confidence of touch.

So acknowledge your male characteristics. Celebrate them. Honor them. Turn them into a manhood that serves the world around you. But do not let them overwhelm you and do not let those who confuse maleness and manhood take your manhood from you. Most of all, do not fall prey to the false belief that mastery and domination are synonymous with manliness.

Be like my father. Be like the generations of nameless men who served as stewards of the age into which they were born and never willingly raised their hands to harm another.

Measure your greatness by the length of your reach, but also by the gentleness of your touch. For now, the world needs hands that love, not hands that conquer. Let your hands be among them.

CHAPTER 3

Strength

T HE OTHER DAY I saw a group of boys pushing against
another boy outside a local store. The lone boy was ges-
turing as if he was going to hit back at his attackers, but you
could see he was afraid. The others kept crowding him and
taunting him and daring him to strike them. Then they were
going to jump on him and beat him. They only needed that
first blow to set them loose.

Finally, an older man walked by and stopped them. The
taunters looked at him and skulked away. The lone boy was
free, but not safe. His attackers will be waiting for him on
another day, in another place.

I don't know what caused this confrontation. I'm sure it
was nothing important. The wrong word, the wrong action.
But from it came a ritual as old as time — boys measuring
themselves by their physical strength.

It's a sad ritual, and not one to make us proud. Yet,
somehow, this notion of physical strength has survived in our
biological coding as something significant, and even the best
of us feel its shudder deep inside us. It is a residue of our days

as hunters and protectors, when our physical prowess was a legitimate measure of our success as men.

Now it is a caricature of all that we need to be.

For ages we have lived with this biological imperative by which manhood has been defined as strength — strength to master others, strength to master our emotions, strength to master the world around us.

Can we lift more, carry more, run faster, work longer than others? Then we are better men.

Can we subdue another person physically? Then we are stronger men.

Can we resist tears when we experience joy or sadness? Then we are truly men of strength.

The world doesn't need this version of strength anymore. We are not locked in some physics of survival where we must turn force against counterforce in an elemental battle to see who will prevail. We need greatness of spirit more than we need greatness of physical strength.

Let me tell you two simple stories. Perhaps you will see what I mean.

Last week I was home alone. I had two tickets to a chamber orchestra concert to be held on Friday night.

I started calling our friends. Those who might enjoy the concert were busy. Those who might be willing to go didn't really like classical music.

The ticket hadn't cost much — I could have just thrown it away and gone alone. But something kept gnawing at me.

For most of the morning I avoided the issue. I tried to ignore the ticket that sat innocently in my billfold. By noon it weighed about a thousand pounds.

Finally, I got in the car and went over to the local nursing home. I went to the nurses' station on the second floor and found the head nurse. "Is there some resident here who can walk a bit, likes music, and wouldn't mind going to a concert with a stranger?" I asked.

The nurses who were standing nearby looked at each other and began discussing various residents. "Edna? Florence? Joe?" After a few minutes they decided that Edna would be the perfect choice. We went to the dining room and asked her. "No, I don't want to," she said. She was afraid.

So we decided on Florence.

We went to her room. She was sitting in her wheelchair with her hands in her lap. She was probably eighty, almost completely blind, and had heavy orthopedic shoes with straps and four-inch soles and laces up the side.

"This young man has tickets to a concert tonight, Florence," the nurse began. "He wants to know if you'd like to go."

I laughed at the nurse's phrasing. "A nursing home is the only place left where I'm likely to be called a young man," I said.

Florence turned her heavy glasses toward me. "Sure," she said. "Let's go. I haven't had a date for a while."

We talked a bit about the concert and the difficulty she might have getting in and out of my car. We set a time when I would pick her up, and I went off about my daily business.

At seven-thirty I arrived back at the nursing home. Florence was dressed and sitting in her wheelchair in the dark. She had on green cotton gloves and was clutching a purse. I said hello to the nurses and off we went.

Everything went smoothly. Florence was able to get into my car. The wheelchair fit into the trunk, if just barely. The people in charge of the concert helped me get Florence into the auditorium and stayed with her while I found a place to park.

Florence decided to stay in her wheelchair during the concert; I had an aisle seat and could stay next to her. Until the lights went down, we talked about people and places we both had in common. While the orchestra was tuning up I read her the concert program — Vivaldi, Bach, Dvořák, and Beethoven.

Then the music began. For an hour and a half Florence sat silently, staring with empty eyes toward a stage she couldn't see and listening to music that she had not heard in years. There was a tiny smile on her lips. She never took off her gloves or let go of her purse.

At the end of the concert, after the applause had died down, she asked if I would get her a copy of the program. "I can't read it," she said. "But I'd like to have one anyway."

There's not much more to the story. I took her home. She thanked me. The nurses joked with her and wheeled her down the darkened hall. Her green gloves were resting on her purse, and under her purse, flat on her lap, was the program.

That's all. Nothing more.

Now, the second story.

One summer when I was just out of high school I worked at a country club with a man named Haines and his son, Calbert. Haines was about sixty and always had a gentle smile on his face. Calbert was in his mid-twenties and wore a slicked-up pompadour and tinted glasses. Because they were black they were required to eat downstairs near the boiler room rather than in the employee lunch area upstairs near the kitchen. I used to bring my food down to eat with them.

"You don't have to do this," Haines would say. "You're not proving nothing."

"I've got to do it because I don't think what they are doing is right," I responded.

"Suit yourself," Haines would say. "Can't do you no harm."

Calbert would just smile and shake his head. "You're just messing yourself up over nothing," he would say as he pulled out the cribbage board. "Nothing you can do about it."

Day by day I would watch Haines and Calbert. I complained to the manager and complained to the other staff. Nothing was changed. Yet, never did I see Haines or Calbert show even the slightest hint of rancor or anger. They just ate their lunch, played cribbage, and went back to work cleaning the men's locker room and shining shoes.

At the end of each day they were given a list of shoes that were to be shined and ready to go the next morning. Sometimes when I would go home Haines and Calbert would still be there shining shoes while the laughter of golfers and their families filtered down from the dining room and lounge upstairs.

At the end of the summer I went off to college, but I continued to visit Haines and Calbert when my travels took me past the country club.

One day I came across an article in our local newspaper.

There had been an attempted burglary at a nearby country club — not the one where Haines and Calbert worked, but another one where I had caddied when I was younger. A black man had been shot and killed after breaking into the locker room with the help of a friend who worked there.

The black man was Calbert.

The policeman who had shot him was a man who had been several years ahead of me in high school. He had been a thug even then; everyone had feared him because he beat up people with chains and tire irons. According to the article, he had claimed that he shot in self-defense, though the bullet had entered through Calbert's back and Calbert had not been carrying a gun. Because there were no witnesses, no case was being filed against the officer.

I was wild-eyed with anger and grief. I went over to see Haines. I found him at his bench shining shoes. "Calbert wouldn't try to kill anybody," I said.

"I know that," Haines answered, putting new laces in a white leather oxford.

"I went to school with that cop," I continued. "He was a thug then and he's a thug now. He just shot Calbert in the back."

"I know that," Haines responded.

"Well, aren't you going to do anything?" I yelled.

Haines looked directly at me. His eyes were clear and sad. "Calbert shouldn't have been there," he said. That was all.

With all the pain he had known in his life, with all the injustice and unfairness that had surrounded Calbert right up to the moment of his last breath, Haines refused to place blame elsewhere. Calbert shouldn't have been there.

I raged and fumed and choked back tears. I couldn't believe what I was hearing. A man had lost his son in an unjustified shooting by a thug in a uniform, and the justice system was turning a blind eye. How could a person be so passive in the face of such unfairness?

Haines just smiled at me and shook his head. "You're angry. I know. I'm angry, too," he said. "That man killed my son. I want to see him behind bars and I'm going to try to put him there. But that don't change nothing Calbert did. Calbert got shot because he was somewhere he didn't belong. Nothing I do is going to make what he did right. He shouldn't have been there."

I stood dumbstruck before this man who had just lost his son. He was obviously filled with pain, but his sense of calm was profound. He did not mount arguments to justify his anger or a hope of revenge. He did not take rash action that would increase the cycle of suffering. He stood in his strength, contained in his grief, secure in the sense of honor with which he lived his life.

In some men this would have seemed like passivity. But one look into the wisdom in Haines's eyes was enough to tell me that this was not a man refusing to act out of fatalism or cowardice. He knew where the moral center of his being was, and he was as strong as a mountain.

I could not have been that strong. I would have flown into a rage and set out to exact some horrible vengeance on Calbert's killer. To outsiders I might have looked like a torrent of righteousness and a tower of strength. But I would not have been as strong as Haines.

Haines, on the other hand, would never have been strong enough to go to that nursing home to ask a stranger to a concert. He accepted the harshness of life and it was not his way to reach out to create happiness for others. He would have let the ticket go unused. He might have congratulated me for my act. But he never would have done it himself. It was not part of his strength.

Two men. Two moments noticed by almost no one. Two very different ways of being strong.

This is important for you to know. Every man has a different strength. A man who chooses to live at home with aged parents, or a man who devotes himself to endless hours of labor to learn the violin or the secrets of quantum physics has a quiet strength that few will ever know. A man who masters his own desire for independence and gives himself over to being a kind and loving father is strong in a way many others could not match, but his strength is never seen.

You need to find your own strength. We have an instinctive tendency to make that false association of strength with force, and to measure it by moments of high drama or grand flourish. We are easily able to see strength when a man climbs a mountain or wards off an intruder. We are drawn to him because he overcame fear, and that is something we readily understand.

But there is much more to strength than overcoming fear. All men are afraid of something. Some fear being hurt in a fight; some fear not having a woman; some fear being embarrassed in front of other people; some fear being alone. Focusing your manhood on your fears and defining your strength by the fears you overcome does not make you strong. It only makes you less weak. True strength lives where fear cannot gain a foothold because it lives at the center of belief.

Martin Luther may have put it most succinctly when he stood up for his vision of God. "Here I stand," he said. "I cannot do otherwise." When you can make this statement about something, all else falls away. You find that your fear is overcome by your belief, your anger overcome by your conviction. Like Haines, you stand in a place of immense peace that cannot be moved, and you possess a strength that is beyond manipulating, beyond arguing, beyond questioning.

Try to find this strength in yourself. It lies far below anger and righteousness and any impulse toward physical domination. It lies in a place where your heart is at peace.

Can you turn and walk from a fight when all those around you are jeering at you and telling you you're afraid? Can you befriend the person nobody likes even though you will be mocked for your kindness? Can you stand up to a group of people who are teasing a person who wants nothing more than to be part of that group? These are the daily tests of a young man's strength.

Can you stay away from a friend's girlfriend even though you want her? Can you turn down a drink or a joint if you don't want one? Can you do these things with kindness and clarity rather than with self-righteousness?

If you can, then you are strong, far stronger than those

who can defeat you physically. Remember, strength is not force. It is an attribute of the heart. Its opposite is not weakness and fear, but confusion, lack of clarity, and lack of sound intention. If you are able to discern the path with heart and follow it even when at the moment it seems wrong, then and only then are you strong.

Remember the words of the *Tao te Ching:* "The only true strength is a strength that people do not fear."

Strength based in force is a strength people fear.

Strength based in love is a strength people crave.

CHAPTER 4

Rainaldi's Lesson

HIS NAME WAS RAINALDI. I was in seventh grade and I think he taught math. We were walking out of an assembly in the school auditorium when I made some smart comment, causing much snorting and laughter among my classmates. Rainaldi looked at me and said, quite gently and clearly, "Nerburn, you start every sentence with the word, 'I.'"

Then he walked away.

If ever a sentence had the power of a koan, that sentence did. With those nine words he changed my life forever.

From that moment forward my perception began to shift. I could no longer look at the world as something that started with me. The self as the focal point had lost its fixed position in my life. Instead, the things I saw, the people I met, the events that filled my day started to become the subjects of my thoughts, and the world opened like a garden around me.

I began the long and still unfinished journey toward seeing the world through the eyes of others, toward knowing the endless joy of entering another's thoughts and feelings and experiencing them as my own.

The change cannot be overemphasized. So often we build our lives around our positions — "I think, I need, I want." Yet the world around us has a life apart from our particular perspective, and we can begin to understand this life more fully if we give over our perspective and see from other points of view.

This may seem abstract, but in fact it is obvious. Our language contains a tyranny of separateness that wears away at our sense of unity like water dripping on a rock. "I see something, I do something" — the "I" stands apart from the world around me, linked to it only by an action. Over time my very language increases my separation and isolation by making me see and understand the world as apart from me. I find myself estranged and alone, and I don't know why.

Other cultures, especially those where "being" is seen to permeate all objects, have unity built into their language. That which they see, not the self, is the natural subject of their thoughts. In ours it is not. We have to make a continual effort to move ourselves out of the center of our point of view.

Very few people ever make that effort. Poets, perhaps, and painters, and artists, and people for whom empathy is a gift of the spirit. But for most of us, the self reigns supreme in both perception and importance.

We need to be shaken from our stance and knocked out of our complacency. We need an epiphany, a koan. Rainaldi gave me mine.

I would wish nothing more than that I could give you yours. But the heart receives such knowledge when it is ready, and your heart will receive it when it is time.

But when it happens, the world will shift in a way you cannot imagine. You will stop trying to find your home in the universe and begin making the universe your home. Judgment will ebb and appreciation begin. Everything will gain the potential to be interesting and beautiful, and every moment will become an opportunity for growth and discovery.

And though you will never completely lose your sense of self — that is the realm of the buddhas and the saints — you will have embarked on one of the most exciting journeys in life. You will have begun to see the world with the heart of an artist, and that, more than anything else, is the secret of keeping the heart eternally young.

CHAPTER 5

Education and Learning

EDUCATION IS ONE OF THE GREAT joys and solaces of life. It gives us a framework for understanding the world around us and a way to reach across time and space to touch the thoughts and feelings of others.

But education is more than schooling. It is a cast of mind, a willingness to see the world with an endless sense of curiosity and wonder.

To be truly educated, you must adopt this cast of mind. You must open yourself to the richness of your everyday experience — to your own emotions, to the movements of the heavens and the language of birds, to the privations and successes of people in other lands and other times, to the artistry in the hands of the mechanic and the typist and the child. There is no limit to the learning that appears before us. It is enough to fill us each day a thousand times over.

The dilemma of how best to educate has always pivoted on the issue of freedom to explore versus the structured transmission of knowledge.

Some people believe that we learn best by wandering

forth into an uncharted universe and making sense of the lessons that life provides.

Others believe that we learn best by being taught the most complete knowledge possible about a subject, then being sent forth to practice and use that knowledge.

Both ways have been tried with every possible method and in every possible combination and balance.

If we find ourselves tempted to celebrate one approach over the other, we should remember the caution of the Chinese sage Confucius, who told his followers, "Study without thinking and you are blind; think without studying and you are in danger."

Formal schooling is one way of gaining education, and it should not be underestimated. School, if it is good, imparts knowledge and a context for understanding the world around us. It opens us to ideas that we could never discover on our own, and makes us one with the life of the mind as it has been shaped by people and cultures we could never meet in our own experience. It makes us part of a community of learners, and helps us give form and direction to the endless flow of experience that passes before us.

It is also a great frustration, because it often seems irrelevant to the passions of our own interests and beliefs.

When you feel burdened by formal education, do not be quick to cast it aside. What you are experiencing is a great surge in your growth and consciousness that is screaming out for immediate and total exploration.

You must remember that all other learners have traveled the same path. And though all true learners have felt this urge to strike out on their own, formal education, in its many shapes and guises, has been sought and revered by all people and all cultures in all times. It has a genius that is greater than your passions, and it is abandoned at your own peril.

Still, formal education will not inform your spirit and make you full. So, along with knowledge, you must seek wisdom. Knowledge is multiple, wisdom is singular. Knowledge is words, wisdom is silent. Knowledge is standing outside, understanding what is seen, wisdom is standing at the center, knowing what is not seen. No person can be whole without both dimensions of learning.

There are many ways to seek wisdom. There is travel, there are masters, there is service. There is staring into the eyes of children and elders and lovers and strangers. There is sitting silently in one spot and there is being swept along in life's turbulent current. Life itself will grant you wisdom in ways you may neither understand nor choose.

It is up to you to be open to all these sources of wisdom and to embrace them with your whole heart.

So do not disparage the lessons of either the schooled or the unschooled.

Those who have less formal education may have learned some single thing more deeply, or they may have embarked early upon the search for wisdom. In their uniqueness, they have discovered something special about life, and it is yours to experience if you are open to what they may have to teach.

Those who have devoted their life to formal learning may have walked further along a path than you can even imagine, and may be able to lead you to a vista that will take your breath away, if only you can overcome your boredom and fatigue at the rigors of the search.

Remember the words of the musician who was asked which was greater, knowledge or wisdom. "Without knowledge," he answered, "I could not play the violin. Without wisdom, I could not play the music."

Place yourself among those who live their lives with passion, and true learning will take place, no matter how humble or exalted the setting. But no matter what path you follow, do not be ashamed of your learning. In some corner of your life, you know more about something than anyone else on earth. The true measure of your education is not what you know, but how you share what you know with others.

CHAPTER 6

Work

I OFTEN HEAR PEOPLE SAY, "I have to find myself." What they really mean is, "I have to make myself." Life is an endlessly creative experience, and we are making ourselves every moment by every decision we make.

That is why the work you choose for yourself is so crucial to your sense of value and well-being. No matter how much you might believe that your work is nothing more than what you do to make money, your work makes you who you are, because it is where you put your time.

I remember several years ago when I was intent upon building my reputation as a sculptor. I took a job driving a cab, because, as I told people, "I want some job that I will never confuse with a profession." Yet within six months I was talking like a cab driver, thinking like a cab driver, looking at the world through the eyes of a cab driver. My anecdotes came from my job, as did my observations about life. I became embroiled in the personalities and politics of the company for which I worked and developed the habits and rhythms of life that went along with my all-night driving shift. On the days when I did not drive and instead worked on my sculpture, I still carried the consciousness of a cab driver with me.

Whether I liked it or not, I was a cab driver.

This happens to anyone who takes a job. Even if you hate the job and keep a distance from it, you are defining yourself in opposition to the job by resisting it. By giving the job your time, you are giving it your consciousness. And it will, in turn, fill your life with the reality that it presents.

Many people ignore this fact. They choose a profession because it seems exciting, or because they can make a lot of money, or because it holds some prestige in their minds. They commit themselves to their work, but slowly find themselves feeling restless and empty. The time they have to spend on their work begins to hang heavy on their hands, and soon they feel constricted and trapped.

They join the legions of humanity who Thoreau said lead lives of quiet desperation — unfulfilled, unhappy, and uncertain of what to do. Yet the lure of financial security and the fear of the unknown keep them from acting to change their lives, and their best energies are spent creating justifications for staying where they are or inventing activities outside of work they hope will provide them with a sense of meaning.

But these efforts can never be totally successful. We are what we do, and the more we do it, the more we become it. The only way out is to change our lives or to change our expectations for our lives. And if we lower our expectations we are killing our dreams, and a man without dreams is already half dead.

So you need to choose your work carefully. You need to look beyond the external measurements of prestige and money and glamour to see what you will be doing on a day-to-day, hour-to-hour, minute-to-minute basis to see if that is how you want to spend your time. Time may not be the way you measure the value of your work, but it is the way you experience it.

What you need to do is think of work as "vocation." This word may seem stilted in its tone, but it has a wisdom within it. It comes from the Latin word for calling, which comes from the word for voice. In those meanings it touches on what work really should be. It should be something that calls to you as something you want to do, and it should be something that gives voice to who you are and what you want to say to the world.

So a true vocation calls to you to perform it and it allows your life to speak. This is very different from work, which is just an exchange of labor for money. It is even very different from a profession, which is an area of expertise you have been sanctioned to represent.

A vocation is something you feel compelled to do, or at least something that fills you with a sense of meaning. It is something you choose because of what it allows you to say with your life, not because of the money it pays you or the way it will make you appear to others. It is, above all else, something that lets you love.

When you find a vocation, embrace it with your whole heart. Few people are so lucky. They begin their search for work with an eye to the wrong prize, so when they succeed they win something of little value. They gain money or prestige, but they lose their hearts. Eventually their days become nothing more than a commodity they exchange for money, and they begin to shrivel and die.

I often think of a man I met on the streets of Cleveland. He was an assembly-line worker in an automobile plant. He said his work was so hateful that he could barely stand to get up in the morning. I asked why he didn't quit. "I've only got thirteen more years to retirement," he answered. And he meant it. His life had so gotten away from him that he was willing to accept a thirteen-year death sentence for his spirit rather than give up the security he had earned.

When I spoke with him I was about twenty. I was young and free; I didn't understand what he was saying at all. It seemed incomprehensible to me that a man could have become so defeated by life that he was willing to let his life die as he held it in his hands.

Now I understand too well. Lured by what had seemed like big money at the time, he had chosen a job that didn't offer him any inner satisfaction. He lived a good life, rolling from paycheck to paycheck and getting the car or the boat that he had always dreamed of having. Year by year he advanced, because businesses reward perseverance.

His salary went up, his options for other types of employment shrank, and he settled into a routine that financed his life. He married, bought a house, had children, and grew into middle age. The job that had seemed like freedom when he was young became a deadening routine. Year by year he began to hate it. It choked him, but he had no means of escape. He needed its money to live; other jobs wouldn't pay him as much as he was currently making. His concern for the health and security of his family kept him from breaking free into a world where all things were possible but no things were paid for, and so he gave in.

"I've only got thirteen more years to retirement," was a prisoner's way of counting the days until the job would release him and pay him for his freedom.

Most people's lives are a variation on that theme. So few take the time when they are young to explore the real meaning of the jobs they take or to consider the real implications of the occupations to which they commit their lives.

Some have no choice. Without money, without training, with the pressures of life building around them, they choose the best alternative that offers itself. But many others just fail to see clearly. They chase false dreams, and fall into traps they could have avoided if they had listened more closely to their hearts when choosing their life's work.

But even if you listen closely to your heart, making the right choice is difficult. You can't really know what you want to do by thinking about it. You have to do it and see how it fits. You have to let the work take you over until it becomes you and you become it; then you have to decide whether to embrace it or to abandon it. And few have the courage to abandon something that defines their security and prosperity.

Yet there is no reason why a person cannot have two, three, or more careers in the course of a life. There is no reason why a person can't abandon a job that does not fit anymore and strike out into the unknown for something that lies closer to the heart. There is risk, there is loss, and there likely will be privation. If you have allowed your job to define your sense of self-worth, there may even be a crisis of identity. But no amount of security is worth the suffering of a life lived chained to a routine that has killed all your dreams.

You must never forget that to those who hire you, your labor is a commodity. You are paid because you provide a useful service. If the service you provide is no longer needed, it doesn't matter how honorable, how diligent, how committed you have been in your work. If what you can contribute is no longer needed, you are no longer needed and you will be let go. Even if you've committed your life to the job, you are, at heart, a part of a commercial exchange, and you are valuable only so long as you are a significant contributor to that commercial exchange. It is nothing personal; it's just the nature of economic transaction.

So it doesn't pay to tie yourself to a job that kills your love of life. The job will abandon you if it has to. You can abandon the job if you have to. The man I met in Cleveland may have been laid off the year before he was due to retire. He may have lost his pension because of a legal detail he never knew existed. He may have died on the assembly line while waiting to put a bolt in a fender.

I once had a professor who dreamed of being a concert pianist. Fearing the possibility of failure, he went into academics, where the work was secure and the money was predictable. One day, when I was talking to him about my unhappiness in my graduate studies, he walked over and sat down at his piano. He played a beautiful glissando and then, abruptly, stopped. "Do what is in your heart," he said. "I really only wanted to be a concert pianist. Now I spend every day wondering how good I might have been."

Don't let this be your epitaph at the end of your working life. Find what burns in your heart and do it. Choose a vocation, not a job, and you will be at peace. Take a job instead of finding a vocation, and eventually you will find yourself saying, "I've only got thirteen more years to retirement," or "I spend every day wondering how good I might have been."

We all owe ourselves better than that.

CHAPTER 7

Possessions

IT HAS HAPPENED several times, but the one I remember best was in Oregon.

I was living alone in a little cabin thirty miles from the nearest town. I had pared my life down to almost nothing; everything I owned I could squeeze into the back of a car. What remained was precious — the winnowing of a life's actions and choices and decisions. It was my history and my hopes — the meaningful artifacts of my past and the things I thought I needed to move me forward.

Letters. Books. A doll made for me by a friend. My typewriter. A camera. A stereo. Photographs and manuscripts and diaries and poems. A favorite bowl and some pots and pans. So little and yet so much.

When I returned from a two-week absence one Christmas, all of it was gone. The papers were torn up, the typewriter was smashed. The camera and stereo had disappeared. The photographs were defaced.

Shards and chunks of my life lay scattered around the house like garbage.

The doll had been torn and ripped and thrown into the wood stove. Someone had defecated on it.

I sat down and put my head in my hands and cried.

It was a sad event. But sometimes life delivers its epiphanies in ugly forms. This vandalism was one of the best things that ever happened to me.

It freed me. Without that break-in I could never have divested myself of half those possessions. They were me and I was them. Without them, mine was a trackless life.

Yet day by day I recovered. The memories behind the letters still remained. The hands that had made that doll lived in my heart. The manuscripts grew in quality in my memory, but opened me up to new creative efforts. The books had mates in the library. Eventually I bought a new stereo and camera.

Life went on and was none the less for the losses. I even felt a certain lightness of being I had never known before.

The thief had been a cruel teacher, but had taught me something about possessions. From that moment forward I vowed that they would never own me; I would own them.

It was a hard-won lesson, but one we all need to learn.

Look around you. Look at your possessions. How many of them have you used in the last week? How many of them have made a difference in your life? How many of them have made you happy beyond the few minutes immediately after you acquired them?

Probably not many.

Yet how many of them would you willingly give away?

Probably very few.

Most of our possessions arrive in our lives almost by accident. A purchase here. A gift there. Gradually, like falling snow, they accumulate around us until they form the basis for our identity. We become them and they become us. We are what we own.

We are full of reasons why we can't give them away: "It came from someone special." "I use it." "I might need it someday." "No one else would appreciate it like I do."

We have reasons why we can't sell them: "I could never get anywhere near what it is worth." "No one else would ever want it."

At every turn we offer excuses that all, ultimately, reduce to, "I want to keep it for myself." We don't even know why.

We can't seem to see that our possessions are really butterflies that turn into caterpillars. They start with the wings of fantasy. We see them as freedom, as happiness. We believe they have the power to change our lives.

We pursue them with energy and excitement — they give us focus and meaning. We are filled with the thrill of the chase.

When we finally get them, they give us a moment of elation; then, like an echo, a feeling of hollowness comes over us. The thrill of ownership grows cold in our hands.

So we begin again, with a new fantasy. And the cycle continues.

Gradually, our lives fill up with the prizes we have sought. We find ourselves weighed down by their presence. We need to store them, keep them working, protect them from thieves. We need to decide whether to share them. We watch them grow old and obsolete and begin to harbor secret ideas about replacing them. One way or another, they pull our minds toward them.

Then, after we own them for a while, they become part of our lives. We wake up one day and find ourselves surrounded by possessions that mean nothing to us but that we can't throw away. They inhabit our lives like stones around our necks. Our freedom is gone; our lightness of being is gone; our sense of creative outreach is gone. In their place is a sense of responsibility and ownership. We are curators of our own cluttered reality.

We long toward freedom, but there is no freedom. The wings of our fantasies have become leaden. Our lives have developed a sense of physical mass, and we are bound to earth like stones.

What are we to do? Unless we want to live lives of day-to-day survival or dedicate our lives to some higher ascetic ideal, swearing off possessions is not going to make us any clearer or wiser. It will only make us obsessed with our own poverty, and that is no better than being obsessed with our own possessions. Neither the self-absorbed poor nor the self-absorbed rich are doing themselves or anyone else any good.

Somehow, we need to find a true measure of value for our possessions so we can free ourselves from their weight without denying them their rightful value.

There is one test we can use: Does a possession help us give more of ourselves to other people? Does its beauty or utility raise our vision of who we are and what we can do?

This test is not clean and simple. It leaves a great deal up to personal conscience. But perhaps that is how it should be. Efforts to establish absolutes in the world, no matter how noble their intentions, have invariably ended in failure.

Who am I to say that a plastic surgeon who saves the faces of children doesn't do his job better because he drives to work in the comfort and silence of a Mercedes? Would I rather that he sat huddled on a street corner with his hand outstretched, so obsessed with filling his empty stomach that he never did anything for anyone? Or would I leave him his skill, but force him into a less expensive car, going to great pains to point out his conspicuous consumption and wasteful squandering of the earth's resources?

The surgeon in his Mercedes is doing good for the world by his own lights. Despite any feelings I may have, it is not my place to judge. There are plenty of people who would question my lifestyle in a world where children rummage through garbage and people starve in the streets.

In a perfect world perhaps we would all see more clearly. But maybe it is enough to hope that each of us will share our talents, and find the balance between greed and benevolence that allows us to live and thrive and help the world around us grow.

The surgeon's motives may not be pure and altruistic. He may want a showy car because it makes a statement about his success, even as he recognizes that it allows him to concentrate better on the tasks he has to perform. But if, in fact, he benefits the world around him, his concern for himself is balanced by his concern for others, and he helps turn the wheel of life in a way that allows others to grow. I may not think this is enough, but I have my own house to keep in order. I leave the surgeon to his conscience; he leaves me to mine.

You, too, must confront your conscience on this issue. You are at a time in your life when the struggle for identity is titanic, and the need to see yourself reflected well into others' eyes is intense. But is having the latest or the newest or the best really important in helping you become someone of value to this world? Is the desire for a certain car or certain clothing really anything more than a desire to present yourself in the most impressive light so that you can increase your status or social importance?

I realize that such things are important to the young, and that self-esteem is the foundation for more significant contributions later in life. But it is important that you are not manipulated by the makers and image creators whose job it is to make you want ever more, ever newer possessions. Their voice makes you misunderstand possessions and get caught in the trap of believing that your happiness resides in the future and your sense of meaning will be increased by the next possession you acquire.

You need to hear past their voice, to the quieter wisdom that says you will value your possessions more if you have fewer of them, and that you will find deeper meaning in human sharing than in accumulation of goods.

You need to get to the point where you ask yourself if a possession will make you a better person, better able to share, better able to give, more willing to reach out to do good in a world that so desperately needs it. If a pair of expensive jeans will do that, so be it. But when you find yourself saying that it can happen only if there is a new pair of expensive jeans every time a new style emerges, you are hiding from the real intentions that are guiding your desires and are allowing yourself to be manipulated by forces that have no higher purpose than to make your present life seem deficient.

You, like me, like the surgeon in the Mercedes, need to look closely at your motives. You need to discover the difference between what is necessary for you to contribute to the world around you, and what you want merely to increase the worth of your own image or to keep yourself from staring in the face of the realities of the life before you.

I can only hope that you look closely at yourself as you begin to seek and accumulate, and that you will raise your eyes above the level of pure desire when you consider the value of the possessions you gather around you.

I want you to know that the pursuit of most possessions is nothing more than that — a pursuit — and that you should give real thought to the object you are seeking before you invest your time and energy in the act of acquiring it.

I want you to know that possessions have made more people unhappy than happy, because they define the limits of your life and keep you from the freedom of choice that comes with traveling light upon the earth.

I want you to know that possessions are chameleons that change from fantasies into responsibilities once you hold them in your hands and that they take your eye from the heavens and rivet it squarely on the earth.

And I want you to know that possessions that increase your own value are empty in comparison to those that increase the value of the lives around you.

But most of all I want you to know that possessions become what you make them. If they increase your capacity to give, they become something good. If they increase your focus on yourself and become standards by which you measure other people, they become something bad. It is in your hands to give them meaning.

Periodically purge yourself. Give away what you don't use. Go on a long trip and take only a single pack. Do something to remind yourself that most of the possessions you thought were important are nothing more than superficial decorations on who you really are.

Find the few pieces of your life that help you live. Value them for the way they help you give. Never forget that if you just accumulate possessions as the logical outcome of pursuing your desires, you will lose your wings to fly.

It will take the horror of a thief in the night to set you free again, and I wouldn't wish that on anyone.

CHAPTER 8

The Miracle of Giving

As I write this, Christmas is approaching. It is my favorite time of the year. For this one brief season we count our money, not to measure our own security, but to see how much we can give. For this one season we look to make others happy and to find our joy in the happiness they receive.

How simple a lesson, but how easily forgotten.

Almost as quickly as the day ends, we once again become takers, measuring our happiness by what we can gain for ourselves. Just days before, we were valuing our lives by the joy we could bring other people. Suddenly, we are back to the practical business of assessing all our actions by how they will benefit us.

What a sad transformation. How can we forget so quickly? Giving is one of our most wonderful and beneficial acts. It is a miracle that can transform the heaviest of hearts into a place of warmth and joy. True giving, whether it be of money, time, concern, or anything else, opens us. It fills the giver and warms the receiver. Something new is made where before there was nothing.

This is what we have such a hard time remembering. We instinctively build our lives around getting. We see accumulation — of status, of money, of recognition — as a way of protecting ourselves and our families, or as our due for being hard-working members of society. Little by little, we build walls of security around ourselves, and we begin to understand the good things in our lives as the things we can lose. Giving becomes an economic transaction — what I give away must be subtracted from who I am — so even the smallest gifts are weighed on the scales of self-interest.

Even when we reach out and give, we often seek notice and praise, so our hearts are really motivated by the praise we will be getting, not by the pure joy of opening to the needs of another. We are locked in a prison of our own self-interest, and we are blind to the fact that our real growth and happiness would be better served by the very actions we resist performing.

The only way to break out of this prison is to reach out and give without regard for the response we may receive.

Each Christmas I rent a Santa Claus outfit and go out on the streets, just to teach myself this lesson anew. In that Santa suit, there can be no subtle playing for self-congratulation or benefit. No one knows who I am. I am simply Santa, the man who gives.

I go into nursing homes, grade schools, hospitals. I stop and talk to kids in parking lots and bring presents to people who need them. Parents pass me notes and make requests, some wanting me to reassure their children that Santa exists, others just wanting me to pay attention to their child.

Once a Jewish family took me aside and asked me to speak to their little boy. He was the only Jew in his kindergarten class. He thought Santa wouldn't care about him because he was Jewish, so he was afraid to come forward when Santa came into his room. I sat with him and his parents and we talked about Hanukkah and giving, and in the end he gave me a hug and said he wouldn't be afraid anymore. It may have been strange theology, but it was good humanity.

Being Santa costs me money, time, and no small amount of grief. One time two teenagers ran a stop sign and rearended my car. Being Santa, I couldn't bring myself to turn them in and press charges on Christmas Eve. But despite every inconvenience it involves, I would not give up playing Santa for anything. I receive too much in return.

People who focus on getting can never understand this. They might think that what I do is praiseworthy. They might even say, "That must make you feel good." What they don't understand is that it is beyond feeling good; it is creating good. It is bringing good into the world where before there was nothing.

Giving is a generative act. When you give of yourself, something new comes into being. Two people, who moments before were trapped in separate worlds of private cares, suddenly meet each other over a simple act of sharing; warmth, even joy, is created. The world expands, a bit of goodness is brought forth, and a small miracle occurs.

You must never underestimate this miracle. Too many good people think they have to become Mother Teresa or

Albert Schweitzer, or even Santa Claus, and perform great acts if they are to be givers. They don't see the simple openings of the heart that can be practiced anywhere, with almost anyone.

Try it yourself. Do it simply, if you like. Say hello to someone everybody ignores. Go to a neighbor's house and offer to cut the lawn. Stop and help someone with a flat tire.

Or stretch yourself a little bit. Buy a bouquet of flowers and take it to a nursing home. Take ten dollars out of your pocket and give it to someone on the street. Do it with a smile and a lilt in your step. No pity, no hushed tones of holy generosity. Just give it, smile, and walk away.

Little by little, you will start to understand the miracle. You will start to see into the unprotected human heart, to see the honest smiles of human happiness, and you will be able to see humanity in places you never noticed it before. Slowly, instinctively, you will start to feel what is common among us, not what separates and differentiates us.

Before long you will discover that we have the power to create joy and happiness by our simplest acts of caring and compassion. You will see that we have the power to unlock the goodness in other people's hearts by sharing the goodness in ours.

And, most important, you will find the other givers. No matter where you live or where you travel, whether you speak their language or know their names, you will know them and become one with them, because you will recognize each other. You will see them in their small acts, because you will recognize those acts, and they will see you in yours. And you will know each other and embrace each other. You will become part of the community of humanity that trusts and shares and dares to reveal the softness of its heart.

Once you become a giver you will never be alone.

CHAPTER 9

Money and Wealth

MONEY RULES OUR LIVES. You can say it doesn't. You can rail against it. You can claim to be above it or indifferent to it. You can perform all the moral and intellectual gymnastics you will. But when all is said and done, money is at the center of our very claim to existence.

Yet money is not of central importance. It has nothing whatsoever to do with the lasting values that make life worth living.

There, in a nutshell, is the dilemma. How do you reconcile yourself to something that is not important but is at the very center of your life?

I have known many different people with many different ways of dealing with money. I have drunk cheap wine with hoboes whose only money was rolled up in greasy wads in their pants pockets, and talked long into the night with stockbrokers who controlled tremendous wealth yet never touched a penny of cash or coin. I have watched wealthy people who would not give away a nickel out of fear that they would be made poor, and poor people who always seemed to have enough to share with others. I have seen the gracious rich, the criminal poor, the hustler, and the saint.

And all of them have one thing in common: The way they deal with money is a result of how they think about money, not of how much money they have.

Money on its most basic level is a hard fact — you either have it or you don't. But on its emotional and psychological level it is purely a fiction. It becomes what you let it become.

Imagine two different men. The first builds his life around his desires — what he sees in advertisements and what he projects he would need to make him happy. He has an internal accounting system that projects the amount of money he needs to meet his desires, and he feels himself poor unless he has that much.

Never mind that fulfilling those desires is not likely to make him happy. That is another story. On the basic level of money, this man feels poor unless he can fill the distance between his present position and his fantasies with the money necessary to bring those fantasies to life. He may be a millionaire, but if his fantasies run into the billions, in his own mind he is poor.

Another person, who sees money as a simple tool of moving through life, will feel comfortable if he has a dollar more than he needs in his pocket, and positively rich if he has ten dollars more than he needs. He has not built his happiness around desires, so he does not have to measure his money according to how far it will go toward fulfilling those desires. He simply has an extra dollar he can spend any way he wants. He may use it to buy a gift for someone. He may throw it into the air. He can do whatever moves him because he feels secure in the money he has.

The difference between these two men does not lie in their actual wealth. It lies in their psychological relationship to money. They may have exactly the same amount of money, but the man who measures his money against his desires will never be happy, because there is always another desire waiting to lure him. The man who measures his money against his needs can gain control over his life by gaining control over his needs. He can put anything left over in service of his desires.

However, there is a dark side to this simple equation. Certain needs have to be met — food, shelter, clothing, and, I would say, an occasional moment of lightness and fun in life. Without enough money to cover these needs, you will never have peace of mind. Even the person who has pared his financial needs to an absolute minimum cannot overcome the grinding oppression of not having enough to eat or not being able to feed his family. When you don't have enough to survive, money becomes the centerpiece of your life. Obsessed with its absence, your heart very quickly fills with desperation and anger.

If you reach this point, and I hope you never do, you have to rise above the desperation and anger, because few people understand it and even fewer want to deal with it. People who have something can never know what it feels like to have nothing. Even if they once had nothing, they can only remember the hardship; they can't reenter that experience of blinding desperation and rage. Those who were never there don't have the slightest idea about the forces swirling inside you. All they see is an angry, desperate man, and that is someone most people want to avoid, not someone they want to help.

If you find yourself filled with the anger and desperation of smothering poverty, you have to rise above it to communicate your hope. You have to reach inside yourself to find your sense of self-worth and your belief that you can and will do better. Then you have to reach out and communicate that belief to those who might be willing to help you.

Remember that the world is full of desperate people. Even people who want to help can give only so much. They will not respond to more than they see. If they see a hungry man, they will try to feed him. If they see an angry man, they will avoid him or try to calm him. If they see a promising man, they will try to help him fulfill his promise.

So, when you are down and need help to survive, you need to be a promising man, not an angry and hungry man. Your desperation and need will only make people uncomfortable, and the help you get will be no more than enough to ward off their guilt. If, however, you display a belief in your own promise, people will be more likely to help you, because most people enjoy helping others fulfill their promise.

Remember, when it comes to defeating the desperation of poverty, your only real friend is work. A handout helps, but only in the most immediate sense. It doesn't diminish your anger and powerlessness. Work — any work — rebuilds the sense of inner worth that desperation takes away. No matter how petty, work establishes the framework for growth and gives you a place to stand as you try to reach for something higher.

So if the burden of smothering poverty comes over you, do not look for money. Look for work. The money will follow, and the rage and desperation that have their hands around your throat will gradually loosen their grip. Then you can begin to move money out of the center of your life and return it to its rightful place as a tool that helps you live a meaningful life.

Don't make the mistake, however, of believing that only crushing poverty can move money to the center of your life. People who accumulate money to insulate themselves from the tyranny of poverty soon find that money fits its hands as easily around the throats of the wealthy as around the throats of the poor.

Even if you have no interest in money — if you want it only so you don't have to worry about it — at a certain point it becomes an abstraction that operates by abstract laws. It accumulates interest, you need to figure out how to invest it, you need to pay taxes according to how much you make, and it becomes a possession with a life of its own. It grows branches and roots and is buffeted by the winds of economic forces that the ordinary person never even notices. You need to tend it like a gardener, and it becomes central in your mind, even though you thought you were accumulating it so you wouldn't have to worry about it.

So, how should you deal with money? How should you strike a balance between giving yourself over to the tyranny of poverty and giving yourself over to the tyranny of wealth?

There are no hard and fast rules. But there are some basic guidelines you should keep in mind.

The first is this: It is as important to learn how to be poor as it is to learn how to be rich.

Financial well-being is, to a great extent, nothing more than a balancing act on the back of circumstance. You can be thrown off at any time. When you are, you land in poverty. If you know how to be poor with dignity and grace, nothing short of massive financial disaster can disturb your peace of mind.

Knowing how to be poor means developing an unerring instinct for the difference between what is essential and what is only desirable. It means knowing how to take control of your life — how to repair and maintain the things around you, how to purchase wisely and well, how not to purchase at all when you do not have the means to do so, how to take joy in the simple pleasures in life. It means not getting caught up in what is lacking, but finding meaning in what you have. It means knowing how to live with style and creativity without basing your life on money.

These are lessons worth learning at any time, but they are lessons you have to learn if you are to survive when poverty comes. People who have never learned how to be poor insist on acting as if they are not poor. They masquerade, they borrow, they live their lives under false pretenses.

They see poverty as a deficiency. They never see its virtues or its wisdom. They never use it as a chance to learn more about sharing or to sort out the meaningful from the meaningless in their lives. When poverty comes into their lives they do anything to hide from it and to hide it from those around them. Their money is their identity, and the loss of their money means the loss of who they are.

If you learn to accept poverty when it comes, it will make you clearer and stronger and more self-reliant. It will make you more appreciative of the simple gifts of life and will keep this appreciation close to the center of your heart. But you must learn to live by its rules. You must learn to embrace the life of limitations it forces upon you.

If you never learn these things, you are forever living on the edge of disaster, no matter how much money you might have. If you know how to be poor, lack of money will never destroy you.

The second guideline about money is this: The greatest enemy of financial well-being is not poverty but debt.

There are massive forces arrayed in the world to tell you of the great benefits of debt. They will tell you that by borrowing you establish your legitimacy in the eyes of lenders. They will tell you that you can have tomorrow's pleasures at today's prices. They will present arguments and inducements that are seductive and convincing. They will dress debt up in a suit and call it credit. But it all comes down to the same thing: You have mortgaged your future to pay for your present, and this is something you don't ever want to do.

Debt is your enemy because it takes away your freedom of movement and the creativity of your options. Yes, debt can make you money because it allows you to invest when the opportunity presents itself. Yes, debt can help you in the present and leave your problems for what you hope will be a better time in the future.

But debt defines your future, and when your future is defined, hope begins to die. You have committed your life to making money to pay for your past, and your spirit cannot take wing. Leave debt to businesses and corporations that have lives of their own. Stay away from it in your personal life. There is no sadder sight than the person with dreams and promise whose eyes have dulled and whose days are spent pushing the heavy wheel of debt toward an endless horizon.

How much better it is to be at zero and to become the man whose step is light because he has one dollar more than he needs in his pocket. When you are at zero, and if you are not driven by fantasies of perceived need, money has no control over you. You are free to make money work for you in your quest to live a meaningful life.

A third guideline about money is this: Money tends to move away from those who try to hoard it, and toward those who share it.

If you are a hoarder, you live with a locked vault in your heart. Nothing can get in, just as nothing can get out. You will be reduced to quickly opening and shutting that vault when you add or subtract money, and others around you will do the same.

The fresh air of free exchange, where opportunity and need and all the complex elements of our human interactions intermingle, becomes stifled. The richness of possibility is replaced by the aridity of control. You will have what you have, your life will be a constant process of accounting, and the unseen and unexpected, which you cannot control, will slowly bleed you of that which you try so hard to protect.

If you are a sharer, you will bring out the sharer in others. Then money will move freely. By sharing, I don't mean squandering, which is nothing more than the mindless spending of money for no other reason than the excitement of watching it flow. By sharing I mean using your money to enable other people to do something meaningful, without regard for whether or not anything will return to you.

If you do this, you open yourself to the endless possibility of exchange and interaction among people who want to help each other, and people will want to return the kindness you show them with the kindness they have to offer.

It is like any other language through which people deal with each other. People who speak the same way tend to find each other. If your money speaks of protection and hoarding, you will find yourself involved with others whose money speaks of protection and hoarding. You will stare at each other with hooded eyes and closed fists, and suspicion will be your common value.

But if you are one whose money speaks of sharing, you will find yourself among people who want their money to speak the language of sharing. And where the language of sharing is spoken, the world is full of possibility.

But perhaps more importantly, if you are a hoarder you will not be a happy person, because hoarders cannot endure loss. Money comes and goes. That is part of its nature as a basis for exchange. Hoarders cannot abide its going. Sharers, on the other hand, are always wealthy in their hearts, even when they are poor, because they see goodness in the passing of money. And more often than not, their sharing kindles the spirit of sharing in others, and the passage of money becomes a mutual gift that enriches everyone.

The willingness to see money go out from them also helps sharers understand another guideline about money: Sometimes you have to lose it to move forward.

People who refuse to lose money on any transaction become tyrannized by their need to win. Perhaps they purchased something at too high a price. Perhaps the world has changed since they acquired it. Whatever has occurred, people who refuse to lose money when they sell something are trapped and cannot move forward. Sometimes the need to move forward is far more important than the need to extract the last penny out of a situation. Sometimes it is more important than extracting any money out of a situation.

I am reminded of an old, curmudgeonly man who lives near us. His livelihood is making doghouses and he lives in near poverty. We live in a very poor part of the country where there is little money for people houses, much less doghouses. Yet this man insists on selling his doghouses for eighty-five dollars, which is far more than people can pay around here. At one point I needed a doghouse. Unaware of his prices, I went over to see him. I told him I could spend seventy dollars. He refused. "Eighty-five dollars is my price," he said, and slammed the door.

Now, when I drive by his house I see his yard crammed with doghouses. His house is falling down. I am sure his poverty is growing. But he will not change his price. He has established a value in his mind that no one shares. His life cannot go forward until he frees himself from his conviction that he cannot take a loss. He is a slave to his doghouses and is building a hardened wall of poverty around himself. He will die surrounded by doghouses, and they will be sold for five dollars apiece at a yard sale.

Learn from the old man. He is fixated on the doghouses, not on what they will enable him to do. He is trying to operate on some principle of intrinsic worth, and he has forgotten that nothing is worth more to anyone else than the value they attach to it. Nothing should be worth more to you than its value in helping you live your life. If you are willing to slough off the past, even at a loss, you keep yourself free and your world continues to grow. If you insist on holding to some abstract valuation, you are held hostage by that possession.

A good Zen exercise would be to send that old man out and have him pay people to take his doghouses, giving them each the amount that he believes the doghouse is worth. Then the man would find out how much he really values the doghouses and would learn how arbitrary his attachment to them really is.

But I'm not concerned with you achieving Zen clarity about your money. I merely want you to know that it is fluid and ethereal and it comes and goes. If you insist that it always go up, and never down, in value, you are committing yourself to a fight against the natural rhythms of inhalings and exhalings, comings and goings, that characterize our life on earth. Money that passes through your hands either comes back to you or it doesn't. Either way your life goes on, and the more important issues of human growth and caring remain.

But if you do insist on trying to always make the most out of your money, there is one last principle you should know:

Money has what I call a "species recognition." It recognizes its own. People who work among nickels make and lose nickels. People who work among dollars make and lose dollars. People who work among millions of dollars make and lose millions of dollars.

If you really want to make money, you have to be among people where it is exchanged on the level that you want to possess it. There are always stories about millionaires who made their money by adding up nickels and dimes. But those people spent their lives in an obsessive fever of minuscule acquisition, and that is no life worth living.

If you want to be a millionaire, better that you learn the rules and skills necessary to participate in the world of millionaires. Then put your talents to use working among them. The people who are making millions are no more talented than the many who are working for dollars, but they are in the arena where money moves in larger multiples and their talents are rewarded in the multiples that are the accepted level of exchange.

So if you want to make money, you do well to be near money. Money goes where money is. You need to rub against it so that it can rub against you.

But no matter how you choose to deal with money, you need to keep one shining truth before you at all times: It is not how much money you have that is important, but how well you let money pass through you to others.

Money is nothing more than a commodity, an agreed-upon abstraction of exchange. It is the spirit of that exchange that animates money and gives it meaning. Great givers, rich and poor, use money to bring light into this world. Great hoarders, rich and poor, use money to close doors between us all.

Be a giver and a sharer. In some unexpected and unforeseeable fashion, all else will take care of itself.

CHAPTER 10

Drugs and Alcohol

I AM SITTING IN A LITTLE CAFE. The man at a table across from me is drinking. His eyes are heavy. He fades for a moment, lists to the side, then jerks himself up. He is on the edge of sleep, yet still he continues.

He seems to be a good man. There is a gentleness in his face. Perhaps he is feeling lonely. Perhaps he is nursing some private hurt. Perhaps he is an alcoholic.

His features are getting puffy from the drinking. His cheeks are slack and his eyes dull. His lips hang like weights.

He raises his hand to the waitress. She brings him another beer. He thanks her, too intensely. She turns away quickly before he is done talking.

It is a sad and poignant scene. No matter how happy this man believes himself to be, loneliness hangs over him like a shroud. He is a man alone, drawing his truth from a bottle.

He is not so different from me. You or I could be him. He is just a person who got trapped by alcohol, one of the great tricksters.

I call drugs and alcohol the great tricksters because they

hide their true faces from our view. They begin by enhancing the ordinary, but end in their own darkness.

This sounds dramatic and full of false alarm. But it's a sad truth that too many learn too late. In fact, when you first feel that rush of clarity from a drug or first find yourself filled with loving warmth from a few drinks, it seems inconceivable that there can be trouble waiting. Your first response is, "There's nothing to fear here. This can be good if I use it correctly. It's excess that causes the problems, and I don't need excess."

But drugs and alcohol are great seducers and deceivers. They offer you the world in a new way, but from that first moment they are at work on your chemistry. And your chemistry has a logic of its own.

Soon, in subtle ways, they begin to own you and demand that you serve their will. And it is only a matter of time until they cause you to harm yourself or other people.

And you never see it coming.

Consider alcohol. A few drinks and the lights become brighter, the colors richer. Your tongue begins to speak from your heart. The world becomes graceful and suffused with a warm glow. You are at peace.

What can be wrong with something that produces such truth and such honesty?

You will never know until the day when it tricks you. And it will. There will come a moment when the alcohol will tell you what to do, and you will follow.

Maybe you'll be lucky. Maybe it will only cause you to utter a hurtful word, or perform some foolish and embarrassing action.

Maybe you'll be unlucky and great harm will be done. Maybe you'll get a girl pregnant because your love seemed so strong and real. Maybe you'll take the life of a friend, because the warmth that surrounded you made you feel that you could drive faster or longer or with less care.

Maybe you will wake up one day to find that you are one of those people alcohol grabs and refuses to let go, demanding that you start each day with a drink, or guiding you through each day with a gnawing hunger until at last you can take the bottle and find the peace that only it contains.

You will never know which of these awaits you. But one of them does. Drinking is a devil's bargain. You get something extra in the present, but you pay for it in the future. And you never know the real price until it is due.

Drugs are even more seductive. They make you think you have control, they deceive you by taking control themselves, and making you the pawn in a great chemical game that the human system is powerless to resist.

They are even more treacherous than alcohol, because at first they seem to offer so much more. Who can deny the thrill of cocaine, the mysticism of peyote and mescaline, methedrine's sense of mastery, or any of the other drug-induced experiences that seem to lift life so far beyond the ordinary?

In my youth, when I did drugs, I always said that they moved my life from black and white to technicolor. They gave me insights that changed me. I was able to step outside myself and see my life for what is really was, and then set myself a new course. I believed I tasted food for the first time, felt the breeze for the first time, truly made love for the first time. All was new and full of joy.

Then slowly, I saw it all turn. Words would escape me. My memory would fail and my mental quickness was gone. I felt vague pains in my body and vague fears overtook my mind. Free time became dead time; I wanted to fill it with drugs, because reality without drugs seemed boring and drab.

I saw my friends who did not do drugs as fearful, their lives as lacking. I could not imagine that they were having the fun I had because they were not seeing the world as I saw it. I found myself hanging out with people with whom I had nothing more in common than the drugs we shared.

Soon a friend died. Other friends began coughing up blood. One lost his mind, and it had been a beautiful mind. He returned to his parents' home where he lives even today lost in wild and terrifying delusions.

To be sure, there are others who are well. Some still even do some drugs. But we were all tainted. Something was taken from us even as something was given to us. We have a knowledge, but it was not without a price. And I don't want you to have to pay that price. The knowledge is there to be gained in other ways.

I don't know how to explain this in a way that will touch your heart. The world is full of slick slogans, like "Just Say No" — slogans meant to simplify and scare and sell abstinence. Everyone who has seen the downside will tell you horror stories calculated to stop you out of fear. But the true issue is much more complicated.

Drugs and alcohol are not, in themselves, dark and abysmal horrors. But they carry the seeds of dark and abysmal horrors, and they plant them in your mind, your heart, your very chemical makeup. No matter how benign they seem, no matter how elevated the experience they create, they are giving you something at the expense of something else. They are a devil's bargain — a promise of power in exchange for a service yet unnamed — and it is up to you if you wish to make that bargain.

I am afraid of that bargain for you, because I do not know what service will be demanded. That I am well and others are well does not mean that there is still not a service to be demanded. And even if we were set free, you may not be. You must not take the risk and sell your future for the present.

I say all this with full knowledge of the "other" truth — that to some people drugs have been sacred, drugs have been medicine, drugs have been the window into other truths; that to some people alcohol is a part of daily life in a civilized and genteel manner, or part of broader rituals of spiritual freedom. But always there is the bargain, even though it may be unspoken or unrecognized.

I do not wish to lie to you. There were moments on peyote when I heard the springs run underground and heard the wind and the trees as a symphony. There were moments making love on drugs when I thought I was going to be transfigured by the beauty. But none of those feelings lasts, and always there was the shadow.

How to say it? Somehow, those moments were illusion as much as insight. Try as I might, I cannot go back to them in my heart, even though they existed.

In my heart and in my mind I can still stand on the tundra above the Brooks Range in Alaska and weep for the most beautiful landscape I have every seen. But I cannot find the moment of truth and insight of the night on peyote when the springs sang to me from beneath the ground. The truth without drugs endures; the truth induced by drugs disappears.

The world contains enough to fill us a thousand times. I would not trade five minutes of being with you for all the brilliance and beauty of all the drugs I ever took. I would not trade a moment of your mother's love for every blissful second spent in the thrall of alcohol, marijuana, cocaine, peyote, or LSD. They have their seductions and their truths, but they do not have the strength of spirit.

And this is where I think truth lies. It takes courage to step across the line into drugs, but it is a courage based on weakness. The hunger for new experience, the desire to reach new heights and depths, is really an admission that the world is not enough. And that admission is ignorant and false.

To see a solar eclipse when the earth goes dark and the birds tuck their heads under their wings to sleep, to see a child born into the world from the body of a woman you love, to hear the silence of eternity as you stand on a windswept mountain pass — these are enough. And the drugs and the alcohol do not increase them; they merely move them further from life and closer to dream. They give them to you in the moment but they take them from you in your memory. They cannot take root and enlarge your spirit.

Do not be seduced by the tricksters. Do not be deceived

by their promises. Health has been given to you. Fineness of mind and fitness of body are yours. If you choose to play with drugs and alcohol, you reach behind a door where darkness has no name.

Better men than you or I have been destroyed by the hand that will not let go.

CHAPTER 11

Tragedy and Suffering

TRAGEDY AND SUFFERING WILL COME TO YOU. You cannot insulate yourself from them. You cannot avoid them. They come in their own season and in their own time.

When they come, they will overwhelm you and immobilize you. You will feel for a time like you can't go on. If you are one kind of person, you will feel like no other human being has ever known the suffering you are going through. If you are another kind, you will feel that your suffering is so small and insignificant compared to the greater sufferings of others that you are being self-indulgent by feeling your own pain.

Don't be duped by either extreme. A person burned by a match does not feel pain any less because someone else was burned in a fire. Your pain and suffering are real because they are yours. You must embrace them and realize that they, too, are a gift of life because they take you out of yourself and, for a moment, make you one with all others who have known loss or pain or suffering.

The great lesson of suffering comes from the fact that it is so much greater than the confines in which we live our daily lives. When all is going well, our world is a small, controlled experience bounded by our daily necessities. Going to the store, finishing a paper, getting new tires for the car, wondering whether the girl who smiled at me yesterday likes me — these are the levels of concern that occupy our daily lives.

When tragedy and suffering come swooping in, they are unexpected, unforeseen, unprepared for. They shatter our tiny boundaries and break our world into pieces. For a time we are living inside a scream that seems to have no exit, only echoes. Those small cares that seemed so important yesterday become nothing, our daily concerns petty.

When we finally reclaim ourselves, as we ultimately do, we are changed. We have been dropped into chaos and nothing is as it was. We look longingly on life as it used to be and wish we had a chance to do things over again.

But we don't. Our lives are unalterably changed, and we will never again be the persons we were before. We have been carried into a larger realm where we see what truly is important, and it is our responsibility to carry that knowledge back into our daily lives. It is our chance to think life afresh.

How we respond to tragedy and suffering is the measure of our strength.

I know a man who was chained to a bed and beaten as a child. He now lives alone in a single room, aligning his shoes perfectly and setting each object in its appointed place every day. He has no friends other than his sense of order, which is nothing more than the warding off of the chaos that whirled around him as a child.

I know another man who survived Auschwitz as a child and stood by as his mother and father were killed. He now devotes himself to making money and living what he perceives as "the good life." "I've suffered enough," he says. "I have a right to try to claim some happiness."

I also know a woman who was taken, blindfolded, at eighteen, to a dingy hotel room in a distant city to have a bloody, scraping, kitchen-table abortion. She dedicated her life to working with cancer patients, perhaps as an atonement for some perceived guilt, perhaps because she understood some broader dimension of suffering.

I can't judge any of these people. They have each suffered deeply, far more deeply than you or I. But they share something in common — they changed their lives in response to the suffering they experienced.

Some people, like my friend with the shoes and my friend with the money, chose to respond to their tragedy and suffering by insulating themselves further. Perhaps they had to; perhaps the scars were so great they couldn't endure another touch of pain such as they had known.

But what of my friend in the cancer ward? She did not deny her pain. She did not run from it. She accepted it, embraced it, and saw how it made her one with others who knew pain and suffering. Because she had felt death inside her, she chose to share herself with others who were feeling death inside themselves.

We need to see these dark moments as moments of

growth. Those who insulate themselves from further pain miss a great opportunity. They miss the chance to use their pain to grow outside themselves and recognize something greater and shared in our human experience.

Maybe your pain is the loss of a girlfriend or the death of a pet. Maybe it is the death of a parent or an accident that maims or a sickness that never retreats. Whatever it is, it is your measure, and you need to look upon it as a gift to help you reclaim what is important in your life.

Remember, though a hurt may seem unbearable and all-consuming at first, with the healing balm of time it will begin to pass. The human being is a surprisingly resilient organism. We impel toward health, not sickness. Your spirit, as surely as your body, will try to heal.

The question you must ask yourself is not *if* you will heal, but *how* you will heal. Grief and pain have their own duration, but when they begin to pass, you must take care to guide the shape of the new being you are becoming. They reduce our lives to chaos, but in return they offer us a chance to rebuild our sense of values and meaning.

So you should not fear tragedy and suffering. From them can come your greatest creativity. No one should seek them, but no one can avoid them. Like love, they make you more a part of the human family. Experience them for what they are, but use them for what they can be.

They are the fire that burns you pure.

CHAPTER 12

Fighting

I ONCE HAD A DOG THAT LIKED TO FIGHT. He would attack other dogs, whether they had challenged him or not. I would curse and scream and try to separate him from his opponent, but he was beyond strength. When finally the fight would be over, I would sit him down and stare at him. Win or lose, his mouth was pulled back in a twisted grin; he was hyperventilating, and his eyes were crazed in an almost beatific way. He had tied into something so deep and dark in himself that he was at peace, even if he was badly injured.

Human beings who fight become the same way. Fighting induces a primitive euphoria in us that has no concern for harm or injury. All of our senses become hyperconscious. We tap into something that courses through the deepest part of our species.

Some men crave this. They never feel more fully human than when they fight. They are oblivious to the harm they do and the harm that is done to them. They love that mixture of fear and anger and see fighting as a noble test of their manhood.

You may know people like this. Surely you know of

them. Lacking any broader vision or sense of purpose, they embrace the physical sensation that fighting gives them. They think fighting is a measure of manhood, and they look down on people who won't fight, thinking they are unmanly.

You must beware of these kinds of people. They will try to convince you of the manliness of their outlook and will try to make you join them. If you refuse, they will goad you and taunt you and prod you and challenge you. They will insult your ego and your family. They will play on your fear.

They will do anything to bring you into their arena of confrontation, because without an adversary they have no identity. They need confrontation to ratify their existence.

You need not engage these people. Your manhood is not on the line. Do not fall prey to their logic that says you are less then they if you choose to walk away rather than fight. Just because you feel fear does not mean that you are a lesser man. They feel fear, too. They just choose to identify their manhood with their capacity to overcome that fear by fighting rather than by some higher good such as the ability to care for the weaker or the ability to express gentleness.

Suppose you were to fight them and win. Would you be more of a man? Of course not, unless you choose to see your manhood as nothing more than the capacity to inflict more violence on an opponent than the opponent can inflict on you. So why should you be less of a man if you choose not to fight or do not manage to win?

You must not let these men define the terms of your life. What you must learn to conquer is not them but your belief that such men somehow represent strength. You must learn to assert the higher human values of goodness and caring over your instinctive sense that fear is weak and conquest is strong. Those are battles that you must fight inside your heart. You can never resolve them through physical confrontation.

Yet, there are times when you may have to fight to protect yourself. Our world is full of irrational violence and desperate people who see fighting as a way to gain control over the world around them. At some point one of them may confront you and leave you no way out.

They may want to fight you because you are big, or because you are little, or simply because you do not want to fight. They may want to fight you out of their own rage or desperation or sense of inadequacy. They may want to fight you simply because you are there. They will not let you walk away and no amount of rational discourse will stop them.

What should you do? I believe you must look upon such people as having a sickness. It is a sickness that corrupts the human spirit by reducing us to our lowest level and violating our impulse toward goodness and caring. When people want to fight you, they are spreading this sickness in the world. It is your responsibility to stop it.

If you can stop the disease without fighting, if you can neutralize it and return it to health through love and compassion or reason and logic, do so. If you can walk away from it with nothing more than a loss of face or ego, do so.

But if a person threatens to harm you or someone you love, or someone who is helpless, like a child or an elder, then I believe you must be willing to fight. If you are not, you are allowing the illness to spread because you are allowing people to be harmed by your inaction.

But when you fight you must do so without anger. You must act with the dispassionate involvement of a physician. A doctor may hate disease, but he is not angry at it. He knows that he must act coolly and without malice, using his best judgment.

Like the physician, you must be clear and decisive. You must remain distant and dispassionate, using the minimal force necessary to bring the fight to a conclusion. Do not be concerned about winning or losing. You have already lost by having to fight. See what must be done to bring the fight to a stop, then do it.

If you find yourself fighting because you want to inflict harm on another person, your fight is wrong. Only when fighting the harm another person might cause can your fight be just. You are seeking a cure; you are not punishing the carrier of the disease.

Remember, though there are many good reasons to fight, there are no good fights. Someone always gets harmed, and when one person is harmed we are all diminished. Rise above your passions and fears and you will be able to avoid most fights. But when a fight finds you, do not see it as a personal issue. Avoid it or undertake it in a way that allows you to walk away from it whole in body and spirit.

As Lao Tzu says, "The best fighters display no anger. The best conqueror seeks no revenge."

If you must fight, that is the way I would want you to do it. Do not become a dog with a twisted face.

CHAPTER 13

War

I HOPE OUR NATION NEVER CALLS upon you to fight. It means the world is out of balance and madness is loose in the land.

But such times come. Then you must choose. It is not an easy choice.

Our society is good to us, by and large. We reap its benefits and generally accede to its requests. We elect the people who make our public policy decisions, and they generally have no more love of war than you or I.

So when our leaders make the decision that we as a society must fight, there usually is a logic behind their decision. They may perceive some growing threat to our way of life. They may see going to war as the only way to advance some policy that they believe is crucial to our survival. They may say that we need to fight to preserve the essence of our way of life.

But you as an individual may not agree with their thinking. You may not believe in the necessity of their policies. You may not believe in the centrality of the values they are defending. You may feel there is no greater threat to our way of life than to leave your children without their father if you were to be killed.

Governments do not want you to make this decision. They deny your right to determine what you feel is a "just" war. They will allow you only the position of pure pacifism — that there is no justification for fighting, not even if your family is threatened.

However, if you are not a pure pacifist — if you would fight to defend you family, but would not fight to defend our country's right to an abundant supply of some resource, for example — the government considers this an invalid stance. It reasons, by extension, that the threat to the resource is a threat to our way of life and hence to your family, and therefore it expects you to fight when called. If you refuse, you will very likely be forced to leave your country or to go to jail.

You must make a decision on how you are going to respond when your country asks you to fight in its name. On one end is the belief that killing is wrong and that you will not participate in it no matter what; on the other is the belief that you are part of a society and that when wiser minds than yours have reluctantly made the decision to fight, you will support their decision.

In between is the vast area of moral, philosophical, religious, political, and tactical disagreement by people who wish to choose other ways.

People of good heart have chosen all paths.

I would counsel you to deal with war just as you deal with fighting in your personal life. Look at the issue of where the sickness is on our planet. Is it in the adversary that our country wants us to fight? Is it in our country's policy and lifestyle? Is it in the general mindset that war is a viable way of settling differences? Where you stand in relation to the sickness is where you should stand in relation to the war.

But do not be too quick to act or judge. It is easy to say that we must assert the high road and begin to establish a new order. But war has always been a part of human experience, and violence is still very much a part of the human character. It is a hollow victory to assert the high moral principles of pacifism while the whirlwinds of violence are storming the gate.

Still, there are those who would stand strong, even at the expense of their own lives, to assert this better part of our nature. They would let those whirlwinds of violence overrun us, believing that good must triumph in the end, and that no good ever came from brother raising arms against brother. These people see the long view, and know that the choices we make in the short run stretch out into our future. They are willing to sacrifice, even their lives and the lives of those they love, to see the vision of a warless society rise up on the horizon.

If you can clearly and honestly say that you are among these visionaries, then your choice is clear. You are a pacifist and you will assert the higher order even if it means death and destruction of all that is good in the short term. Great people — Martin Luther King, Mohandas Gandhi, Mother Teresa — have taken this stand.

But before you embrace this position, ask yourself, will I stand by and see my family killed by wanton violence if it comes to that? Do my principles lie that deep?

If, on the other hand, you believe that any war declared by our country is a just war because our country is an honorable, if imperfect, society, then you can assert the higher order of patriotism and fight whenever the country asks. Great men have done this, even to the sacrifice of their own lives on lonely battlefields filled with unmarked graves.

But then ask yourself, am I willing to die and leave my children without a father so that my country can have cheap gasoline or a ready supply of some other resource? Is my commitment to my country's well-being that strong? Am I willing to follow a country fevered by war, even when no motive other than revenge is being served? Am I willing to kill the child of another man to advance an abstract principle that my government has decided to assert?

If not, then you are left in the middle, having to decide if the war is a just war. How should you decide?

I will give you a possible guideline.

There is a Chinese story about a group of learned men who were sitting around a well discussing whether there is such a thing as good and evil. As they were talking, an old man walked by. "Let's ask him," they said, and they put the question to him. The old man thought for a moment, then pointed to the well. "If you see someone throwing a baby down that well," he answered, "you know there is something wrong."

This seems simple, but you need a simple rule in such complex circumstances. When society or a government is killing children, you know something is wrong. A sickness is abroad on the earth, and it must be stopped before it spreads.

If our government is killing children to secure some abstract gain, then our government is wrong and ought to be opposed. If another government is killing children and our government sees fit to try to stop them by warfare, then you can feel that the war is just.

Other wars are based on more or less false premises. Wars fought to settle arguments over political, economic, or religious systems are nothing more than fights of childish arrogance. Wars fought over control of property and resources are nothing more than the offspring of greed and fear. Wars fought to end oppression or to alleviate crushing poverty are more problematic. But by and large they are false wars because innocent people are being killed, even though the purpose of the particular war may be noble in the abstract.

Therefore, we come back to the killing of children. Is the fighting worth the death of an innocent child? Hold that child's life in your hands. Will you sacrifice it to achieve the goal or the policy our country is pursuing? If the goal is to eliminate a madman who may kill hundreds or thousands of others, perhaps you will say yes. Such madmen rise up with alarming frequency, obliterating their people with force or famine. Occasionally a maniac rises up who threatens us all. Occasionally entire nations are swept into a frenzy of violence and loose a conflagration that threatens to engulf a part of the earth. Perhaps, in such cases, you will decide that saving many is worth the death of a few.

But always, look carefully. Your government will try hard to justify its position. It will threaten you and it will obfuscate. It will present you with stories and images that have the sole purpose of convincing you to follow its chosen path. Truth will become a victim long before there are any bodies lying on the ground. When this happens, you must search your heart. You must seek the wisest counsel you can, and the wisest counsel is always found by listening to the most considered arguments of all points of view. Try to learn the truth, then stand by the truth you have learned.

If that means fighting, do so honorably. If that means resisting, do so with courage. Whatever you choose will have harsh consequences, for war has always been and will always be a madness. That it came in your time, and caused you and your generation to respond, is a burden that you can neither choose nor escape. You can only stand firm in the center of your heart and respect those of all positions who have chosen to stand firm in the center of theirs. When the fighting is over, and it will be over, you will all be brothers and sisters in time, and it will be your shared responsibility to pass the world on to the generation that follows.

Just remember: There is no war to end all wars. Warfare is always the lowest way, and it is always the way that leads to death. Warfare should be called for, and your life should be asked for, only when the greatest of perils to human life is alive in the land.

When the evil is so great that you are willing to see children die, then you should be willing to fight. If you are not, you should turn your hands to the ways of peace.

The Spiritual Journey

W E ARE ALL BORN WITH A BELIEF IN GOD. It may not have a name or a face. You may not even see it as God. But it is there.

It is the sense that comes over you as you stare into the starlit sky, wondering what is out there. It is the morning shiver as you wake on a beautiful day and smell a richness in the air that you know and love from somewhere you can't quite recall. It is the mystery behind the questions you ask when you wonder what was before the beginning of time or what is on the other side of the end of space.

It is a sense of otherness.

Some people will tell you that there is no God. They will claim that God is a crutch for people who can't face reality, a fairy tale for people who need myths in their lives.

They will argue for rational explanations for the origin of the universe and scientific explanations of the perfect movements of nature. They will point to evil and injustice in the world, and cite examples of religion being used to start wars or to hurt people of different beliefs.

You cannot argue with these people, nor should you. These are the people the Chinese philosopher Chuang Tzu spoke about when he said, "A frog in a well cannot be talked to about the sea."

If you have any sense of the mystery of the universe around you, you are hearing the murmurings of the sea. Your task is to leave the well, step out into the sun, and to set out for the sea. Leave the arguing to those who wish to discuss the size and shape of the walls that close them in.

But choosing to leave the well is not easy. In an attempt to explain the great mystery we call God, people have put forth different stories, different pictures, and different truths. Too often these seem to be naive or grotesque or at war with one another.

How do we embark on a path when the paths we see around us end in a God with a great white beard, or offer religions that subjugate women, terrify children, and tell us that those who hold different beliefs are damned? How are we to accept paths surrounded by mythologies and filled with more judgment than love?

If you are one who hears the murmur of a distant sea, do not be turned away by the naivetés and contradictions of the beliefs around you. Those beliefs have their place for people who can gain by them. There are many paths to the sea, and the sea looks different from each of them. Your task is not to judge the paths of others but to find a path you can walk.

But how are you to choose a path?

Most of us were either raised in a tradition that strictly defined a single path, or we were left alone to find our own way by parents who were too unsure to force a single path upon us.

Those of us who were raised the first way at least know how to believe, but we don't know how to seek. We may know the sea is there, but we may not believe in the path that was pointed out to us, so we stand still, unable to move. Those of us raised the second way are free to seek, but we don't know how to believe. We stare longingly at the many paths, but are not really able to step firmly upon any of them.

We are immobilized — surrounded by those who don't seek at all, intimidated by those who seem to have found a quick and easy path that contains no doubt, and haunted by the endless murmurings of the mystery that calls to us and won't let go.

We must begin by accepting where we are. We all have special gifts of character. Some of us are blessed with compassion; others, laughter; others, a power of self-discipline. Some of us are filled with the beauty of people, others with the beauty of nature. Some of us have a keen sense of the injustices in life; others are drawn to celebrate the goodness around us. These are all starting points, because they are all places of belief. You must find the gift that you have — the source of your belief — and discover a way to cultivate that gift.

I sometimes like to think of God as a great symphony and the various spiritual paths as instruments in an orchestra. The gift that you have is like music waiting to be played. You need only to find the instrument that will best bring it out. You alone can never play all the instruments, and your music might not find voice in all instruments. All you can do is find the instrument that suits you best, play it as well as you can, and add your music to the great symphony of divine creation.

I once spent several months living in a Benedictine monastery in British Columbia. I was making a sculpture for the monks, so I sought to partake of their spiritual vision. It was an austere vision calculated to bring those who practiced it to God by immersing them in a spiritual rhythm of work and prayer until the self was burned off like a husk, leaving only the Benedictines' centuries-old rhythm of faith and belief. It was, for lack of a better term, a confrontation with the Big Gods, where the self becomes like a weak cry in the distance until it is heard no more.

I did not like Benedictine spirituality. Its timbre was too dark. But the abbot, who was an astute man, pulled me aside one time and said, "Stay in the machine. It will clean you out."

He was right. Though I barely touched the surface of their belief, like a tourist passing through a foreign land, I began to be taken up to the Big Gods of their truth. I was opened to a great spiritual vastness where there were no distant campfires, but only the great, restful darkness of union. I began to hear the celestial music made by the perfectly tuned instrument of Benedictine spirituality. Had I stayed, I am sure I would have soon become part of that music.

But Benedictine Christianity was not my instrument, and I turned back from it as soon as my time in the monastery was through. My spiritual music was different, and I needed to find a different instrument on which to play.

Nonetheless, I had glimpsed their truth, and it was a beautifully crafted instrument for the spirit. That I did not choose to learn to play it, or to let it play me, is not to make it any less beautiful or real. It has its part in God's symphony, and the orchestra would be the lesser if the great voice of Benedictinism were not there to be heard.

If you come upon a tradition that seems to give voice to the music of your spirit, do not be afraid to follow. Religious traditions exist because they give voice to fundamental spiritual truths that many people share. They offer a path to the sea that has been taken before, and their footsteps are well marked for those who choose to follow. If you find a tradition that engages your spirit, give yourself to it with your whole heart. Read its texts. Participate in its rituals. Give yourself over to its ways of spiritual formation.

But, if you find that your faith in God is something silent and personal found in the solitude of your own heart, do not be afraid to embark upon that path. Seek out the wisdom of the mystics and the visionaries who met their God face to face, and cultivate the habits of the heart that will allow you to grow closer to the experience of God every day.

But always remember this: Spiritual growth is honed and perfected only through practice. Like an instrument, it must be played. Like a path, it must be walked. Whether through prayer or meditation or worship or good works, you must move yourself in the direction of spiritual betterment. Spiritual understanding never deepens unless you subject yourself to the spiritual discipline of practicing your belief.

Even so, there will be times when you will feel you have

lost your way. You will be too tired to go on, or other things will seem more important. Maybe you will start to feel that your belief was just a momentary enthusiasm. Maybe you will feel a growing meanness of spirit. Maybe you just won't care.

Don't be too hard on yourself when this happens. Your whole life is your spiritual journey, and you will find yourself in arid lands as well as in lands rich in possibility. Once you begin, you will never turn back. Just be certain that you continue to push forward.

Most of all, have faith in your path. Follow it as you can; change it if you must. But do not give up the search for the sea. As you get closer, the murmur gets louder, and your certainty of its existence will grow. You may not find yourself on the path you expected, but you will be on a path nevertheless.

Perhaps you will find yourself believing in God as a concept, perhaps as an ordering principle. Perhaps your belief will lead you to God as a being, or as an experience of undifferentiated unity. But wherever it leads you, it will lead you somewhere.

The Buddhists have a story about blind men trying to describe an elephant by feeling its various parts, and each describes the elephant according to the part he touched. That is the way we can hope to know God.

Do not refuse to seek God because you cannot find the one truth. We live in a pluralistic world, and only the most hard-headed refuse to accept the fact that truth — whether spiritual, cultural, political, or otherwise — is given to different people in different ways. Find the path that glows like a sunlit day, rich in remembered scents and promises. Then follow. Only a fool refuses to walk in the sunlight because he cannot see the shape of the sun.

CHAPTER 15

Loneliness and Solitude

YOU SHOULD SPEND TIME ALONE. I don't just mean minutes and hours, but days and, if the opportunity presents itself, weeks. Time spent alone returns to you a hundredfold, because it is the proving ground of the spirit.

You quickly find out if you are at peace with yourself or if the meaning of your life is found only in the superficial affairs of the day. And if it is in the superficial affairs of the day, the time spent alone will throw you back upon yourself in a way that will make you grow in wisdom and inner strength.

This is no small discovery. We can easily fill our days with activity. We buy, we sell, we move from place to place. There is always more to be done; there is always a way to keep from staring into the still pool where life is beyond the chatter of the small affairs of the mind. If we are not careful, we begin to mistake this activity for meaning. We turn our lives into a series of tasks that can occupy all the hours of the clock and still leave us breathless with our sense of work left undone.

And always there is work undone. We will die with work undone. There is no sense in trying to defeat the labors of life. They are endless. Better that you should accept the rhythms of life and know that there are times when you need to stop to draw a breath, no matter how great the labors are before you.

Though this may sound mystical and abstract, the universe has an eternal hum that runs beyond our individual birth and death. It is a hum that is hard to hear through the louder and closer noise of our daily lives. It is the unity that transcends us all and, as much as possible, reconciles us to the reality and inevitability of our deaths. It makes us part of something larger.

This knowledge can only be experienced fully in solitude.

For many people, solitude is just a poet's word for being alone. But being alone, in itself, is nothing. It can be a breeding ground of loneliness as easily as a breeding ground of solitude. Solitude is a condition of peace that stands in direct opposition to loneliness.

Loneliness is like sitting in an empty room and being aware of the space around you. It is a condition of separateness. Solitude is becoming one with the space around you. It is a condition of union.

Loneliness is small, solitude is large. Loneliness closes in around you; solitude expands toward the infinite. Loneliness has its roots in words, in an internal conversation that nobody answers; solitude has its roots in the great silence of eternity.

Most people fear being alone because they understand

only loneliness. They feel that unless the world presents them with a mirror in the form of another person responding to them, they are close to annihilation.

Without their own reflection they become afraid, even frantic. The world is comfortable to them only as long as they are the center of their understanding. When they are alone, nothing ratifies their existence because no one responds to them.

Solitude is about being at peace with the fabric of existence. It is about getting the "I" out of the center of your thoughts so that other parts of life can be experienced in their fullness.

All this takes place in the still, clear space where we cease to think in words and our hopes and memories cease to define the limits of our thoughts.

Some people are closer to this space than others. Some have already found it through hours of reverie in their childhood. Others have discovered it through enforced loneliness that somehow burst forth into a sunshine of understanding. Others have spent their lives in frantic activity and have never even known it exists. But we can all reach it.

We just need to carve for ourselves that space in time when no one can get to us and no one can take us out of the largeness of our reverie. As you become older, surrounded by family and responsibility, this becomes harder and harder, if not impossible. But as a young person, you need only to claim that time as important for itself and go off to the places where the emptiness echoes and the silence sings.

Though these places can be found anywhere, nature is

the clearest bringer of solitude. Even in the company of others, nature's greatness can overwhelm the insignificant chatter by which we measure most of our days. If you have the wisdom and courage to go to nature alone, the larger rhythms, the eternal hum, will make itself known all the sooner. And when you have found it, it will always be there for you, wherever you find yourself. The peace without becomes a peace within, and you can return to it as you need it, because you know where to find it in your heart.

For most of us the search involves a grinding of the gears as we slow from hurried to quiet to still to peaceful. We have to pass through a period of loneliness where minutes hang like weights in front of us and we bang frantically against the edges of our thoughts.

But it is worth the struggle. Slowly, inexorably, we emerge into the ultimate quiet of solitude. It is like stepping forth into a multihued garden of flowers and scents. We are miles from the sharp edges and harsh scratchings of daily affairs. Our lives breathe anew.

We are in a place where we are beyond thoughts — where we hear each sound and feel each heartbeat; where we are present to each change of sunlight on the earth around us, and we live in the awareness of the ongoing presence of life.

In this awareness the whole world changes around us. A tree ceases to be an object and becomes a living thing. We can smell its richness, hear its rustlings, sense its rhythms as it carries on its endless dance with the wind. Silence becomes a symphony. Time changes from a series of moments strung together to a seamless motion riding on the rhythms of the stars. Loneliness is banished, solitude is in full flower, and we are one with the pulse of life and the flow of time.

This awareness is priceless for the peace it can give. But it is also the key to true loving in our relationships. When we have a part of ourselves that is firm, confident, and alone, we don't need another person to fill us. We know that we have private spaces full of goodness and self-worth, and we grant those we love the same. We do not try to pry into every corner of their lives or to fill the emptiness inside us with their presence.

People who don't know solitude never understand this. They are obsessed with the loneliness in their lives. They make unrealistic demands on those they love because they look to them to fill this loneliness. In the name of love they smother those around them with their needs and expectations. They demand total absorption as part of a relationship, and they fear the freedom of those to whom they try to give their love.

In fact, what they want is for the people they love to conform to the shape of their own emptiness. The spaces in their lives, which should be rich, private sanctuaries, are really nothing more than vast longings waiting to be filled. The love they give becomes a bondage, and they never understand that their intentions, which are so pure, are sucking the life out of those for whom they care most.

To be truly happy in life, you must learn the lesson of solitude. It is not hard to learn. You must only learn to be still. You must resist the restlessness and the chatter and the clutter until you can break free into the space where time has no measure and longing ceases to exist. Be patient. Be accepting. Solitude is a place you reach, not a decision you make.

As always, look at the world around you. The mountain is not restless in its aloneness. The hawk tracing circles in the sky is not longing for union with the sun. They exist in the peace of an eternal present, and that is the peace that one finds only in solitude.

Find this place in yourself. Go to the places where solitude reigns. Drink in the lessons of the great silences, and you will never know another moment of loneliness in your life.

CHAPTER 16

Sports and Competition

I F AT ALL POSSIBLE, you should participate in sports. Though they are often subject to criticism by people who see only their worst side, sports allow you to learn some lessons about yourself that cannot be learned so well in any other way.

Sports of any sort have several unique characteristics. First, they are profoundly finite. They are bounded in space and time; they have a definite beginning and ending. Unlike so much of life, you know how well you have done when they are over. In this concreteness they are deeply satisfying. You have walked into a created world, measured yourself by a standard, and been given immediate results. There is no waiting for knowledge and meaning, no sense of the world being completely mutable and subject to interpretation.

In sports, there is a winner and a loser, a faster or slower time, a higher score or a lower. Everything is laid out before you in the time that it takes place. In a way that almost no other experience offers, sports provide you with a little slice of reality, precise and measurable, set apart from the rest of daily life and completely contained within itself.

Because they are a part of life but set apart from it, sports develop a kind of hyperreality in memory. Ask anyone about a certain game they played in, even if it was years ago, and they will be able to remember a moment as vividly and crisply as if it had occurred yesterday. Something about the contained nature of the event combined with the heightened physical exertion and sense of vigilance gives sports a brighter hue than everyday reality. Other activities do this, but sports are one of the most immediately accessible and available.

Sports also offer you a unique arena in which to exercise your intelligence and will. Usually the physical dimension in any sport is simple. One person is stronger, or you are limited by your physical capabilities. But invariably you can compensate with your intelligence for your physical limitations or deficiencies. Learning to play smart is a reward in itself, and learning that intelligence can overcome physical dominance is a lesson that all of us would do well to learn.

Yet there are times when the opposition's physical dominance is too great to overcome. This is when you find out about your will. Can you stand up to inevitable defeat and continue to struggle? Can you force yourself to excellence when failure is inevitable? Can you find inner satisfaction in outward defeat?

These discoveries get to the heart of sports. They allow the moral dimension of a person's character to be revealed through the physical. Such words may sound grandiose, but they speak to some very real discoveries that even the most unreflective athlete makes.

Are you a person who wants to win or are you a person

who doesn't want to lose? Are you a person for whom anger is a prod to greater accomplishment or does your anger cause you to act against your own best interests? Do you strive to excel at the expense of those around you or do you find your sense of excellence in helping those around you be their best? Do you try to overcome something by challenging its strength or looking for its weakness?

In the actual arena of competition, you make these decisions immediately and instinctively. You do not have time to think them out. It is only after the event that you can really see what you have done. Rather than thinking yourself into existence, you have acted yourself into existence.

I once knew a man who ran the mile as a competitive event. Every morning he would get up, run stairways and hills, do squats and sprints and leg lifts, and subject himself to a training regimen that sometimes left him weeping in pain. To the best of my knowledge, he had never won a race.

One day I was at a track with him while he was working out. He had just finished running a training mile, and was bent over, almost retching.

"Why do you do this to yourself?" I asked. "I don't see you getting any joy from it."

He walked back up the track to a point about ten yards before the finish line, then drew a line in the cinders with the toe of his shoe.

"Why do I run the mile?" he said. "I do it for these last ten yards. In these last ten yards I learn more about myself than I could on any psychiatrist's couch."

In that one sentence, he had isolated one of the most

profound reasons to participate in sports: "the last ten yards." Every sport has them, whether they be in the form of the last few minutes of a game or the last few inches of a putt. They are the moments when the body and the will are tested to the fullest.

There is a case to be made that we humans are most fully revealed at the moments when we are most fully tested. Whether you are talented or supremely ungifted, in "those last ten yards," you take the measure of your own character.

For all these reasons, you should find a sport you love and give yourself over to it. If you are able to participate for the sheer joy and self-understanding that it offers, and if you can avoid the trap of confusing athletic accomplishment with the celebrity and notoriety that it can bring, you will be rewarded with a sense of camaraderie with others and insights about yourself that are hard to achieve any other way.

Most of all, when you meet another person who is going through "the last ten yards" in some aspect of their own life, you will have compassion for what they are experiencing, because you will know what the experience of "the last ten yards" entails.

The arena of competition will have increased your capacity for compassion. And any activity that can do that, especially while increasing your own physical health and self-understanding, should be sought out and cherished as one of the true gifts of life.

CHAPTER 17

Travel

I HAVE NEVER MET ANYONE who didn't at least once feel the lure of the road and the call of distant spaces. Wanderlust, the urge of adventure, the desire to know what is over the next hill are like echoes in the backs of our minds that speak of sounds not quite heard and places not quite seen.

For some these echoes are distant and small. They are easily put aside in favor of the closer, more immediate pursuits of building a life and a home and a family. For others they are as loud as the sea and never go away, no matter how strong the desire to settle and build.

I believe you should listen to these echoes when you are young. Take the chances and follow the voices that call you to distant places. Live, if only for a short time, the life of a traveler. It is a life you will always cherish and never forget.

Let me tell you about a moment in my life. Maybe it will help you understand.

The snow had been falling steadily since morning. As we reached the last checkpoint, it was coming down in blinding sheets.

Ahead of us the Brooks Range loomed like a great black wall, shrouded in fog and mist and whirling torrents of snow.

"It's snowing like hell up there," the man at the checkpoint hut said. He cradled his rifle in his arm. "We'll be shutting her down for the winter any day now."

I looked at the narrow gravel roadway stretching off from the checkpoint into the fog. Maybe it was passable. Maybe not. This roadbed had been hastily carved out for the construction crews that built the Alaska pipeline between Fairbanks and Prudhoe Bay. It was nothing more than a hogback of gravel that cut a forlorn line across the jagged landscape of the Alaska wilderness. Makeshift white crosses had been pounded into the roadbed where tanker drivers had lost control of their rigs and had plunged to their deaths. Now we were standing at Disaster Creek, the last stopping point before the Brooks Range and the tundra. After the heavy crags of the Brooks, there was no human habitation for a hundred and fifty miles until the scattered trailers and Quonset huts of Deadhorse and Prudhoe Bay.

I walked up to a tank-truck driver who had just come through the pass. His truck was covered in ice.

"Can we make it?" I asked.

"You got chains?"

"No," I responded.

"I wouldn't try it," he said.

I told the others. They overruled me. "We came this far. We're not turning back."

Reluctantly I climbed into the van and we started our ascent. The van slipped and fishtailed as we started up the gravel pass. Soon we were pushing through a blinding snow-storm. We could see nothing ahead of us, and the narrow road had no guardrail to the right. A truck hurtling toward us out of the whiteness, a slip of the rear wheels, and we would slide off into a precipice where our bodies couldn't even be retrieved. Six dead. Six white crosses. Nothing more.

The driver gunned the engine and shot forward into the dim halo of his headlights. He couldn't slow down because we might not get started again on this icy gravel. If we stopped, we could not back up, because the road was too narrow and the traction too unsure. We would be stranded on a mountain pass where grizzlies roamed the rocky slopes and there were no human voices for a hundred and fifty miles.

Several times the driver almost missed a curve and the wheels spit gravel over the edge into the snowy darkness as he jerked us back onto the roadway.

No one said a word. We all sat listening to our heartbeats and gripping the corners of our seats. I was white with terror, convinced we were going to die. This time, I told myself, I had made a mistake. This time I had gone too far.

Then, abruptly, we broke through the storm. The mountains stretched out on either side of us. Ahead, far in the distance, was the greatest plain I had ever seen in my life. Like some vision of ethereal whiteness, it was so vast that you could see the curvature of the earth. We dropped from the pass toward this endless expanse. Terror had been replaced with exhilaration.

We made our way down onto this limitless land and pulled to a halt.

The great mountain winds had ceased. We stepped out into a haunting silence. The earth rolled and undulated before us like a great snow-covered sea. The sky was suffused with a perpetual purple twilight that made the land seem frozen in time.

The scale and rhythm of the landscape were dizzying. I felt unsure of my balance, uncertain whether the next rolling valley was a hundred feet away or ten miles in the distance.

Far to my right stood a mountain range that arched from one end of my vision to the other. It was like a crown upon the horizon, with snow-tipped points that disappeared into the opaline sky.

I could not find my bearings. The silence was so loud that it seemed celestial, the landscape so vast that boulders seemed to be pebbles. Billows of lavender-tinged clouds floated like mountains in the gloaming sky to the north. I could not tell where the earth ended and the sky began. I was in a dream world too large for my own imagining.

I circled around and around, wanting to take it all in. But the scope was too great. When I had set out on my travels I had expected to see beauty, but nothing like this. I could not claim this experience; it could only claim me.

I was no longer myself. New truths rushed in on me like great winds. Colors I had never seen and spaces I had never felt washed over me and took me to unknown regions of my spirit. I was giddy and disoriented. My old self had been sloughed of like a false skin and in its place stood someone new, larger, unknown to me.

I would never again be the same.

This is the magic of travel. You leave your home secure in your own knowledge and identity. But as you travel, the world in all its richness intervenes. You meet people you could not invent; you see scenes you could not imagine. Your own world, which was so large as to consume your whole life, becomes smaller and smaller until it is only one tiny dot in time and space.

You return a different person.

All you need to do is give yourself over to the unknown. It doesn't have to be on a vast, dreamlike arctic plain. It can be on a gentle stroll through a Wisconsin forest or on a street corner in Nairobi. What matters is that you leave the comfort of the familiar and open yourself to a world totally apart from your own.

Slowly memories of the familiar recede from your mind and you find yourself adrift in the experience of the world around you. Your thoughts and concerns change. Your emotions focus on new people and events. The world makes its claim on your heart and mind, and you are free, at least momentarily, from the concerns of your everyday life.

Many people don't want to be travelers. They would rather be tourists, flitting over the surface of other people's lives while never really leaving their own. They try to bring their world with them wherever they go, or try to re-create the world they left. They do not want to risk the security of their own understanding and see how small and limited their experiences really are. They move from hotel to hotel, protected by money and credit cards, and never really meet the world through which they are traveling.

To be a real traveler you must be willing to give yourself over to the moment and take yourself out of the center of your universe. You must believe totally in the lives of the people and the places where you find yourself, even if it undermines your faith in the life you left behind.

You need to share with them, participate with them. Sit at their tables, go to their streets. Struggle with their language. Tell them stories of your life and hear the stories of theirs. Watch how they love each other, how they fight each other. See what they value and what they fear. Feel the spaces they keep in their lives.

Become part of the fabric of their everyday lives and you will get a sense of what it means to live in their world. Give yourself over to them — embrace them rather than judge them — and you will find that the beauty in their lives and their world will become part of yours.

When you move on, you will have grown. You will realize that the possibilities of life in this world are endless, and that beneath our differences of language and culture we all share the dream of loving and being loved, of having a life with more joy than sorrow.

But travel is not as romantic and exotic as it sounds. The familiar will always call, and your sense of rootlessness will not give you rest. Your emotions will fly crazily in all directions until sometimes you will feel that you have lost your moorings. If you travel alone, the warmth of families and couples will break your heart, and your loneliness will plunge you to depths you did not think possible.

And then, there are greater dangers. You may wake up

and discover that you have become a runner who uses travel as an escape from the problems and complications of trying to build something with your life. You may find that you were gone one hour or one day or one month too long, and that you no longer belong anywhere or to anyone. You may find that you have been caught by the lure of the road and that you are a slave to dissatisfaction with any life that forces you to stay in one place.

These things happen. But how much worse is it to be someone whose dreams have been buried beneath the routines of life and who no longer has an interest in looking beyond the horizon?

I believe it is worth taking the risk. How else will you know the feeling of standing on something ancient, or hearing the silent roar of empty spaces? How else will you be able to look into the eyes of a man who has no education, never left his village, and does not speak your language, and know that the two of you have something in common? How else will you know, in your heart, that the whole world is precious and that every person and place has something unique to offer?

And when you have tragedies or great changes in your life, how else will you truly understand that there are a thousand, a million ways to live, and that your life will go on to something new and different and every bit as worthy as the life you are leaving behind?

These lessons and more will have etched a new element in your character. You will know the cutting moments of life, where fear meets adventure and loneliness meets exhilaration. You will know what it feels like to almost run, but instead to stay. You will have come to the edge of a precipice and jumped, so you will always know what it means to say yes or no when another jump confronts you in your life.

These lessons and memories will remain with you always, and will serve as a comfort and a guide as you go through your life.

As I sit here now, I can return to that dreamlike plain in northern Alaska. I can sit at tables with Italian marble workers and drink warm wine that tastes like sunlight. I can watch the women with their purple velvet baby carriages converse on the streets of Brooklyn. I can see the lightning flying upward from the ground on a September night in the high Montana desert.

But more than that, because I have traveled, I can see other universes in the eyes of strangers. Because I have traveled, I know what parts of me I cannot deny and what parts of me are simply choices that I make. I know the blessings of my own table and the warmth of my own bed. I know how much life is pure chance, and how great a gift I have been given simply to be who I am.

And when I am old, and my body has begun to fail me, my memories will be waiting for me. They will lift me and carry me over mountains and oceans. I will hold them and turn them and watch them catch the sunlight as they come alive once more in my imagination. I will be rich and I will be at peace.

I want you to have that peace, too. There is nothing sadder than the person who one day looks up at a life of empty effort and wasted days and asks, "What have I done?"

That is why we need to travel. If we don't offer ourselves to the unknown, our senses dull. Our world becomes small and we lose our sense of wonder. Our eyes don't lift to the horizon; our ears don't hear the sounds around us. The edge is off our experience, and we pass our days in a routine that is both comfortable and limiting. We wake up one day and find that we have lost our dreams in order to protect our days.

Don't let yourself become one of these people. The fear of the unknown and the lure of the comfortable will conspire to keep you from taking the chances the traveler has to take. But if you take them, you will never regret your choice. To be sure, there will be moments of doubt when you stand alone on an empty road in an icy rain, or when you are ill with fever in a rented bed. But as the pains of the moment will come, so too will they fall away. In the end, you will be so much richer, so much stronger, so much clearer, so much happier, and so much better a person that all the risk and hardship will seem like nothing compared to the knowledge and wisdom you have gained.

I once wrote a traveler's blessing in one of my journals: "May you have warm shoes, a soft pillow, and dry clothes." That's all. With the closeness of those simple goodnesses, one can dream of the stars.

CHAPTER 18

The Blue Moment

I WAS TWENTY-FIVE, penniless, alone, frightened, and ill, living in a small garret in the medieval university town of Marburg, Germany. I had no friends and I was far from family. My days were spent working in an antique restoration shop owned by an embittered alcoholic man, and my nights were spent wandering the streets watching the passing lives of people who neither spoke my language nor knew of my cares.

I had never been so alone.

The mother of the man for whom I worked was a very wise woman. As a child of twelve she had watched as the Nazis came into her classroom and took the Jewish children away. No one had spoken of it and class had gone on as if nothing had happened. But day by day, night by night, she saw her friends and playmates disappear.

She became a watcher and a survivor.

For months she watched me struggle with the turmoil inside me. She would see me sitting with the neighborhood children in the shadow of the castle, drawing cartoons. She would see me staring vacantly into the distance when I thought no one was watching.

Then, one day, she took me aside.

"I watch you," she said. "I see the loneliness in your eyes. I watch your heart running away. You are like a lot of people. When life is too hard they try to look over the difficulty into the future. Or they long for the happiness of the past. Time is their enemy. The day they are living is their enemy. They want to die to the moment. They live only for the future or the past. But that is wrong."

"I have a simple rule," she continued. "Seek always the blue moment."

She sat down beside me. "The blue moment can happen any time or any place. It is a moment when you are truly alive to the world around you. It can be a moment of love or a moment of terror. You will know it only in memory. My childhood classmates are dead, but I have the blue moment when we looked in each other's eyes."

I turned and stared into her lined and gentle face.

"Listen carefully to me," she continued. "This is a blue moment. We will never forget it. At this moment you and I are closer to each other than to any other human beings. Seize this moment. Hold it. Do not turn from it. It will pass and we will be as we were. But this is a blue moment, and the blue moments string together like pearls to make up your life. It is up to you to find them. It is up to you to make them. It is up to you to bring them alive in others."

She brushed her hand through my hair and gave me a pat on the side of the head.

"Always seek the blue moment," she said, and returned to her work.

Now, years later, my friend Frau Dupont is dead. Cancer took her after we had passed through each other's lives. But I can never forget her words. I no longer judge a moment by the pleasure or pain it contains. Instead, I look to give myself over to that moment in a way that fills my heart and spirit.

I know that if I abandon my own needs and expectations, the blue moment will come. I have had blue moments while my heart was broken. I have had them when I was sitting idly drinking a cup of coffee listening to the birds outside my window. I have had them while talking with complete strangers. They come on like torrents of grace, unexpected, unannounced, suffusing life with a warmth and truth that will live forever in my memory. They are the gift of the spirit.

You must learn to court the blue moments in life. They truly are pearls of great price. You cannot force them. You cannot manufacture them. But you can call them if your heart is still and you give yourself totally to the present moment.

But you will never find the blue moments if you seek to judge or measure events by how they benefit you or how they contribute to your happiness. If you do this, you are starting your understanding at the self, and the self is limited by your expectations and awareness. Only if you give yourself over to the richness of the universe can the self be lifted and transfigured. Then, and only then, can the blue moments happen.

Try to follow Frau Dupont's advice. When you are alone, far from home, look for the blue moment. When you reach over to touch the face of someone you love, look for a blue moment. When you are stopped on the street by a crazy person whose eyes are wide and whose words make no sense, look for the blue moment. It is there. It is waiting for you.

I know only a little about Zen. But I believe the blue moment is what Zen is all about. It is a gift of the universe to those who let themselves be subsumed in the beauty and fullness of the moment, and do not seek to judge life by how the world treats them or by measurements of happiness and gain.

Frau Dupont was like a Zen moment passing through my life. She gave me a simple lesson that illuminated the world around me.

"Always seek the blue moment." If I can pass this on to you, I pass on one of the purest and simplest keys to happiness that life has offered me.

CHAPTER 19

Craig's Lesson

Most young people I know — and many who are older — live in a quiet crisis of identity about their place in the world.

Some, especially young women, spend their lives submerging their interests into the interests of others until they are not sure whether they have any identity at all.

Others, very often young men, try desperately to impress others by parading their accomplishments and sense of self-importance in an attempt to make themselves seem somehow whole and finished. Still others of both sexes spend their time passing a brittle judgment on others they perceive as different or lesser than they are in an attempt to establish their own identity at the expense of others.

At the heart of each is the fear that someone else might pass judgment on who they are, and that they will be unmasked or found out for the uncertainty that is at their core.

When I was younger I was as plagued with this fear as anyone else. Often I dared not act for fear of someone judging me. Other times I forced myself into the center of discussions in a pitiful attempt to make sure I was recognized for everything I thought or did. I excluded others; I demeaned others; I pointed out their weaknesses and inconsistencies as a way of raising myself by lowering those around me. Sometimes I was aware of it; other times I was not.

It took a chance comment by a friend of mine, long after I had reached adulthood, before I could begin to lift myself out of the uncertainty that surrounded my sense of self.

Craig was a close friend of mine. He was one of those people who brought energy and life into any room he entered. He had an uncanny ability to focus his entire attention on you while you were talking, so you suddenly felt more important and more responsible than you had before he started listening. He made you better by being around him. People loved him.

He and I went to graduate school together. We had a lot in common. We both were having women troubles. We both were seekers. We both were perhaps too aware of our own foibles for our own good. But he lived in the sunlight of the spirit while I lived under a full moon. We were like mirrors to each other, revealing dimensions of our beings that otherwise we never would have seen.

One sunny autumn day we were sitting in our study area, half-talking and half-working on some now-forgotten projects for our graduate degrees. I was staring out the window when I noticed one of my professors crossing the parking lot. He had been away all summer, and we had not parted on good terms. I had taken great offense at some suggestion he had made, and had in turn given great offense in my answer. We had not seen each other since that day.

"Damn it," I said to Craig. "I don't want to see him."

"Why not?" Craig asked.

I explained what had happened the previous spring. "We left on bad terms," I said. "Besides, the guy just doesn't like me."

Craig walked over and looked down at the passing figure. "I think you've got it wrong," he said. "You're the one who's turning away, and you're just doing that because you're afraid. He probably thinks you don't like him, so he's not acting warm toward you. People are like that. They like people who like them. If you show him you're interested in him, he'll be interested in you. Go down and talk to him."

Craig's words smarted. I walked tentatively down the stairs into the parking lot. I mustered my best smile and warmest feelings, and greeted my professor and asked how his summer had been. He looked at me, genuinely surprised at my warmth, and put his arm over my shoulder. We walked off talking. Out of the corner of my eye I could see Craig at the window, smiling.

It was so simple, yet I had never seen it. I was approaching all my encounters with a fear that others were judging me when, in fact, they were afraid I was judging them. We were all living in fear of being judged by the other, while the empty space between us was waiting to be filled by a simple gesture of honest caring.

"People like people who like them." Those words allowed me to see the world through new eyes. Instead of seeing judgment in the eyes of others, I saw need. Not deep yawning need, but the simple human need to be noticed and cared about. I began to realize that most people were not waiting to judge the adequacy of my actions; they were waiting for the chance to share something about themselves.

Craig knew this. He basked in people as if basking in sunlight. Their lives warmed him and they loved sharing themselves with him. That was what made him so special.

From that day forward I turned my life around. It was not easy. I still spent too much time fearing the judgment of others. And I still got hurt when arrogant people took advantage of my openness and used it either to laugh at me or to demean me. But I found that by taking the chance and liking other people, the world opened up before me.

I discovered a world of people I never would have known had I kept only to my own interests. Car mechanics, cashiers, crazy people, thieves — all had their stories to tell. The wealthy, the poor, the powerful, and the lonely — all were as full of dreams and doubts as I was.

Farmers talked to me about tractors, scientists spoke to me about atoms. I learned what it is like to grow up on the Australian coast, and I learned how it feels to pack boxes all day long. One time on a train through Canada, I began talking to a man everyone was avoiding because he was weaving and slurring his speech as if he was drunk. It turned out that he was recovering from a stroke. He had been an engineer on the same line we were riding, and we talked long into the night while he regaled me with the history beneath every mile of track: Pile O' Bones Creek, named for the thousands of buffalo skeletons left there by Indian hunters; the legend of Big Jack, a Swedish track-layer who could lift 500-pound steel rails; a conductor named McDonald who kept a rabbit as his traveling companion. When we parted, he said, "Thanks for talking to me. Most people wouldn't bother." He didn't have to thank me. The pleasure had been all mine.

On a noisy street corner in Oakland, California, a family who stopped me for directions turned out to be from Australia's isolated northwest coast. I asked them about their life back home. Soon, over coffee, they regaled me with stories of huge saltwater crocodiles "with backs as wide as car hoods" near their home.

Each encounter became an adventure, each person a lesson in life. The wealthy, the poor, the powerful and the lonely, all were as full of dreams and doubts as I. And each had a unique story to tell, if only I had the ears to listen.

An old, stubble-bearded hobo told me how he'd fed his family during the Depression by firing his shotgun into a pond and gathering up the stunned fish that floated to the surface. A traffic patrolman confided how he'd learned his hand gestures by watching bullfighters and symphony conductors. And a young beautician shared the joy of watching residents in a nursing home smile after receiving a new hairstyle.

How often something like this is waiting to happen. How often people sit in their silence, longing for a chance to tell their stories. The girl who everyone thinks is ugly, the boy with the odd clothes or the strange manner — those people have stories to tell, as surely as the most popular, most successful, most attractive people do. As surely as you do. And like you, they dream that someone is willing to hear.

If you are the one who reaches out, if you are the one who dares to like other people, the walls around you will fall away. Those whose attention you crave will turn toward you because you are turning your attention to them. Those who are alone or insecure will value you for having taken a chance to hear their stories. You will find yourself more valued and respected than you ever could be by parading your accomplishments and sense of importance before other people, because you will have given other people a chance to shine. And far from being lost in their shadows, you will be reflected in the light of their happiness and increased sense of self-worth.

That is what Craig knew. It was the reason he filled every room with warmth and energy. He brought people alive because he cared about them more than he cared about their opinions of him. He took a chance and liked people without first asking if they liked him or if they were worthy of being liked. He generated the good feeling that filled the space that separates people.

Being a person like Craig takes courage. People will accuse you of all sorts of manipulations and false motivations. They will question your associations and take advantage of your openness. But nothing they can do or say will take away the sense of adventure that comes from enlarging your interest in the people and life around you. No accusations they can make will take away the security that comes from knowing that your life is made richer by every person you meet.

Take a chance. Like people first, ask questions later. See if it doesn't open the world to you in a new way. See if the light you shine on others isn't reflected back on you a hundred-fold.

CHAPTER 20

The Power of Art

L AST NIGHT WAS NEW YEAR'S EVE. A rerun of Leonard Bernstein conducting Beethoven's Ninth Symphony in the Berlin Spielhaus on New Year's Eve, 1989, was on television.

I remembered reading about it when it happened. It was an extraordinary concert for an extraordinary time. The Berlin Wall had fallen. People in Eastern Europe were alive with a joy we in America can only imagine. The atmosphere was heady, intoxicating, giddy with the thrill of freedom.

Musicians had gathered from the Soviet Union, the United States, and all over Europe for the performance. Choirs had been massed from around the world.

Leonard Bernstein had been asked to conduct. There he stood, a Jew who had lived through the dark years of the Holocaust, in the midst of the city that had symbolized both the Nazi regime and the division of the world into the camps of communism and democracy, preparing to lead an orchestra and chorus from the nations of the world in a song of healing and celebration.

He was also dying.

What a valedictory for a man who had given his life to the joy and power of music. The faces of the orchestra members, the beaming of the children in the choir, the quiet, intense electricity of those in the audience all spoke of an event beyond our imagining.

All was coming together: the great vision and horror of the Germanic genius, the triumphant victory of the human spirit over the power of politics; Beethoven in his majesty, Schiller's powerful poetry of freedom; the memory of the death camps, the unity of a people too long divided; the old year — the old epoch — giving way to a new as walls crumbled and a great surge of long-suppressed human emotion swept across the globe.

Bernstein raised his baton and it all came pouring forth — the joy, the sadness, the power and the majesty — rising over the ghostly memory of six million dead and the anguish of years of exile for the human spirit.

The instruments sang with one voice. The music rose and expanded and became pure emotion.

Tears streamed from my eyes. I wept uncontrollably. It was more than I was, and more than I could ever be. It was a healing and a testament to the best of who we are and the worst of who we are. It was confession, it was celebration. It was us at our most human.

By the time the concert was over, I had been transformed. Into my daily life had come a moment of sheer beauty. Though at an electronic distance, I had been in the presence of one of those moments that only art can provide, when we humans bring forth something from nothing, and invest it with a majesty and beauty that seems to rival the visions of the gods.

This is the power of art. It lives in music, it lives in theater, it lives in painting and architecture and sculpture. It can come in the words of a poem or on the pages of a novel.

I can measure my life by the moments when art transformed me — standing in front of Michelangelo's Duomo Pieta, listening to Dylan Thomas read his poetry, hearing Bach's cello suites for the first time.

But not only there.

Sitting at a table in a smoky club listening to Muddy Waters and Little Walter talk back and forth to each other through their instruments; listening to a tiny Japanese girl play a violin sonata at a youth symphony concert; standing in a clapboard gift shop on the edge of Hudson Bay staring at a crudely carved Inuit image of a bear turning into a man.

It can happen anywhere, anytime. You do not have to be in some setting hallowed by greatness, or in the presence of an artist honored around the world. Art can work its magic any time you are in the presence of a work created by someone who has gone inside the act of creation to become what they are creating. When this takes place time stands still and, if our hearts are open to the experience, our spirits soar and our imaginations fly unfettered.

You need these moments if you are ever to have a life that is more than the sum of ordinary daily affairs.

If you can create these moments — if you are a painter or a poet or a musician or an actor — you carry within you a prize of great worth. If you cannot create them, you must learn to love one of the arts in a way that allows the power of another's creation to come alive within you.

Once you love an art enough that you can be taken up in it, you are able to experience an echo of the great creative act that mysteriously has given life to us all.

It may be the closest any of us can get to God.

CHAPTER 21

Women and Men

IT WAS A HEADY SUMMER. I was young, American, and living in Italy. My roommate was Iranian. He was a quiet man who labored under some deep private burden. He even called himself Camillo because he did not want people to know he was Iranian. We slowly became close and began to spend our time together.

The Italians have a custom of promenading around the town in the heat of early evening. People put on their best clothes and go to the local squares or fountains where they drink Campari or stroll with their friends. It is a time of conversation and friendship, not to mention gossip and courtship.

One evening Camillo told me his friend Reza was going to come with us for the evening promenade. Reza was loud and frantic and always full of fun. He was a great character for laughter but too often a fool when serious issues were discussed.

We began our promenade as the moon rose over the dusky Tuscan hills. It was one of those electric nights when the outlines seem almost too clear and even the most ordinary street becomes a carnival.

Ahead of us walked three women, arm in arm, as is the manner in many European countries. Reza grabbed me by the wrist and breathlessly whispered, "Watch this!" He ran up to the women and quickly did a somersault on the ground right in front of them. He looked like nothing so much as a monkey doing tricks in a zoo.

The women stepped back and stared at him. He let out a great laugh and ran back to us chattering something in Iranian. Camillo was staring at the ground. "What the hell were you doing, Reza?" I asked, astounded.

"Oh, women," he said. "They love that kind of thing."

Reza was wrong. Women do not love that kind of thing. They may occasionally be flattered by it, if they are in the right mood. But they do not love it. It turns them into objects of sexual pursuit and makes our relationship with them into an embarrassing spectacle of sexual cat and mouse, with us playing the part of a most ridiculous cat.

Few of us act as absurdly as Reza did. But we do often act in a fashion that reduces women to objects. You can see it everywhere: men in pickup trucks, businessmen in elevators, young guys standing on street corners — whistling at women, yelling at them, staring at their bodies and making nudges and comments — generally assuming a right to familiarity with women just because they are women.

It's sad to see, and it's embarrassing. All this cheap, hard talk is ultimately nothing more than a mask for our desperate fascination with women.

This fascination is natural. Women are at the center of our lives from our earliest days. They haunt us and intoxicate us and infuriate us. We love them, we hate them, we want them, we want to not want them. At our best we try to deal with them as equals. But somewhere in all our relationships is the echo of sexual difference that we cannot deny.

These echoes may be real, but they cannot form the basis of our relationship to women. For centuries — probably forever — women have been laboring under expectations determined by our sexual difference. Now their dissatisfaction has burst forth in common voice. Women have forced their issues out into the light, and we all must look at them for what they are.

We men cannot set the agenda. It is impossible for us to understand the biological imperatives of being a woman and the psychological realities of a life spent seeing yourself mirrored in the glances of men. It is impossible for us to know the frustration that can fill a person whose life is defined at its upper limits from the moment of her birth, and who is told from the beginning that her role in the world is somehow colored by her sexual identity.

For us to presume that we can define the limits of women's lives, or even subtly define our relationship to them as a shadow of our own fascination and desire for them, is to feed the fires of anger that have been built up over a very long time.

We, as men, need to get out of the way while women explore the areas of life that have been so long denied them. At the same time, we need to search our own hearts to find out if we carry the traces of attitudes and preconceptions that have driven women to the point of frustration and anger. We need to find the Reza inside each of us, to see where we have demeaned women without intending it, and where we have acted toward them as women first and human beings second.

Eventually, when the waters clear, we need to work together with women to find a way to be partners when we need to be partners, and to be lovers when we need to be lovers. We need to find common ground where we can agree on the significance of our differences and unite on the common issues of our humanity.

This is not going to happen easily. Right now no one knows how to draw the lines on what we have in common and where we have legitimate differences, and what all of this means.

We all — men and women alike — see the opposite sex through two sets of eyes. Part of us sees just the human being. Another part sees the mysterious "other" that animates the whole tangle of desire and love and sexual tension.

We have to learn how to deal with this dichotomy. The current urge toward equality between men and women, while long overdue, has the subtle side effect of proclaiming an identity between us. And we are not the same. If we don't yet know the nature and significance of our differences, it doesn't mean they don't exist. We are, at once, the equals of each other as human beings, and the opposite sides of a physical and, maybe, emotional and spiritual equation that together forms the whole of the human experience. To deny this fundamental difference is as destructive as denying our fundamental similarity.

We need to keep an eye to this mystery even as we fight to claim our commonality. Men are not women; women are not men. The dynamic between us will always be there. The challenge is to find a framework where this dynamic can find full expression without subjugating women beneath the expectations of men and without asking men to define themselves in response to the expectations of women.

You are part of a generation that has a chance to do this. You have a chance to define a new kind of manhood. If you do it well, it will be a manhood in which men do not cheapen themselves and the women around them by the kind of casual, brittle talk that turns women into objects and sex into sport. It will be a manhood in which men see the effects of their gestures and words and most well-intentioned actions. It will be a manhood that does not lead men like Reza to think their monkey-man dance is something women like.

But it will also be a world where we men do not have to apologize for the biological and emotional complexity of who we are, and where we are not held to subtle standards of behavior based on our sexual identity.

In other words, it will be a world where we can love together, laugh together, and work together without fear and without judgment; a world of celebration, not a world of accusation and apology and unexamined assumptions.

This sounds like a tall order, and it is. But it has to start somewhere. That somewhere is in the pickup trucks and in the elevators and on the street corners. It is in the hearts and minds of you and your friends.

Women are already doing their part, and they are finding it a rough go. Now men have to begin, and it will be no easier for us. But it's a struggle whose time has come. One of the lessons of history is that we don't get to choose our issues; our issues choose us.

The issue has chosen you.

Your challenge is to meet it like a man, not like a monkey.

CHAPTER 22

Falling in Love

IT IS A MYSTERY WHY WE FALL IN LOVE. It is a mystery how it happens. It is a mystery when it comes. It is mystery why some loves grow and it is a mystery why some loves fail.

You can analyze this mystery and look for reasons and causes, but you will never do any more than take the life out of the experience. Just as life itself is something more than the sum of the bones and muscles and electrical impulses in the body, love is something more than the sum of the interests and attractions and commonalities that two people share. And just as life itself is a gift that comes and goes in its own time, so too, the coming of love must be taken as an unfathomable gift that cannot be questioned in its ways.

Sometimes — hopefully at least once in your life — the gift of love will come to you in full flower, and you will take hold of it and celebrate it in all its inexpressible beauty. This is the dream we all share. More often, it will come and take hold of you, celebrate you for a brief moment, then move on.

When this happens to young people they too often try to grasp the love and hold it to them, refusing to see that it is a gift freely given and a gift that just as freely moves away. When they fall out of love, or the person they love feels the spirit of love leaving, they try desperately to reclaim the love that is lost rather than accepting the gift for what it was, then moving on.

They want answers where there are no answers. They want to know what is wrong with them that makes the other person no longer love them, or they try to get their lover to change, thinking that if some small thing were different love would bloom again. They blame their circumstances and say that if they go far away and start a new life together their love will grow.

They try anything to give meaning to what has happened. But there is no meaning beyond the love itself, and until they accept its mysterious ways they live in a sea of misery.

You need to know this about love, and to accept it. You need to treat what it brings you with kindness. If you find yourself in love with someone who does not love you, be gentle with yourself. There is nothing wrong with you. Love just didn't choose to rest in the other person's heart.

If you find someone else in love with you and you don't love her, feel honored that love came and called at your door, but gently refuse the gift you cannot return. Do not take advantage, do not cause pain. How you deal with love is how love will deal with you, and all our hearts feel the same pains and joys, even if our lives and ways are very different.

If you fall in love with another, and she falls in love with you, and then love chooses to leave, do not try to reclaim it or to assess blame. Let it go. There is a reason and there is a meaning. You will know it in time, but time itself will choose the moment.

Remember that you don't choose love. Love chooses you.

All you can really do is accept it for all its mystery when it comes into your life. Feel the way it fills you to overflowing, then reach out and give it away. Give it back to the person who brought it alive in you. Give it to others who seem poor in spirit. Give it to the world around you in any way you can.

This is where so many lovers go wrong. Having been so long without love, they understand love only as a need. They see their hearts as empty places that will be filled by love, and they begin to look at love as something that flows to them rather than from them.

In the first blush of new love they are filled to overflowing, but as their love cools they revert to seeing their love as a need. They cease to be someone who generates love and instead become someone who seeks love. They forget that the secret of love is that it is a gift, and that it can be made to grow only by giving it away.

Remember this, and keep it in your heart. Love has its own time, its own season, and its own reasons for coming and going. You cannot bribe it or coerce it or reason it into staying. You can only embrace it when it arrives and give it away when it comes to you. But if it chooses to leave, from your heart or from the heart of your lover, there is nothing you can do and nothing you should do. Love always has been and always will be a mystery. Be glad that it came to live for a moment in your life. If you keep your heart open, it will come again.

CHAPTER 23

The Mystery of Sex

B Y NOW PERHAPS you have already made love with a
woman. If you haven't, you know that your body is cry-
ing out to you with a hunger that you can hardly endure. You
have reached the age where the desire for a woman controls
your every waking thought and colors the way you look at
even the smallest part of your world.

You are no different from any other young man. This is
the way it was for me; it's the way it will be for your son. It's
the way it always has been, and the way it always will be.

What is this force? What are you to make of it and how
are you to make your peace with it?

There are no simple answers.

Sex is a mystery bigger than all of us. It is one of those elemental parts of our being that lies deeper than our individuality, deeper even than our species. It is the generative force that
drives our earth, and maybe drives the entire universe.

So no amount of thought, no amount of reasoning, can
prepare you for that first moment when you enter a woman's
body with your own. In one act you become a different per-

son. Suddenly and irrevocably your entire life begins anew. Your boundaries are changed. Your knowledge of life is changed. You become part of something far bigger, far deeper, than you can imagine.

Once you cross this threshold you can never turn back. You can never stop wanting the feeling that you have experienced, and you are forever in search of a woman to fill that hunger.

This is when sex becomes confusing. Because sex is a real, physical hunger, it can never truly be sated. We can quench the hunger for a moment, but soon it returns, as strong as ever.

Many men allow themselves to be driven by this hunger. They follow their desire for one woman until it is filled, and then they turn their sights to another woman, because their hunger for her is stronger. The physical sensation of sex, the always astounding sense of discovery that comes from entering a new lover's body, drives them from partner to partner in a search to keep the edge of wonderment and joy that comes with the first moment of sexual sharing.

Some of these men are just sexual predators. But many others are well-intentioned. They believe so strongly in the totality and beauty of the sexual experience that they feel honor bound to move on when the incandescent moment of first sexual discovery begins to lessen. They feel that true love can be recognized by total, all-consuming passion, and they do not want to settle for anything less.

They are courting a very great danger. Though they may love women deeply, they cannot sustain their love without the total enrapturing physical sensation that comes with first knowledge and necessarily cools and changes over time. They are drunk on the mystery of the physical, and spend their life fruitlessly chasing that initial moment of complete intoxication.

Other men — though far fewer — court a different danger. They are drunk on the mystery of the spiritual. They sense the eternity and sacredness of sex and demand that these sensations be the center and core of their sexual experience. For them the woman is the repository of the mystery. As soon as their sexual partner becomes a person with hopes, problems, and personal characteristics, these men lose interest because she is no longer a purely spiritual experience.

Both kinds of men do harm to women and to themselves through their sexuality. The first kind loves women because they offer him a chance to become lost in the all-consuming immensity of the passionate moment. The second kind loves women because they offer him the chance to become lost in the all-consuming immensity of an eternal truth. It is quite easy for both types of men to see their sexuality as healthy and holy and a great, loving celebration of the mystery of life.

But both types of men ultimately deny the humanity and individuality of the women they love. What each is really seeking is an all-consuming event that obliterates their self-consciousness. The woman is ultimately the agent of this obliteration.

Even if these men are filled with the deepest gratitude toward the women they love, they are somehow directing that gratitude not to the woman herself but to the beauty and mystery of women in general. Their real gratitude is for the existence of the feeling women evoke in them, not for the woman in whose arms they have momentarily found that feeling. The actual woman they are loving is really nothing more than a vehicle to a sensation, and as soon as she fails to induce that sensation, she becomes an insufficient partner and is discarded.

Such men live in a misery of hopeless expectations, and in the process they dehumanize the women on whom they place these expectations. They wander blindly in their passionate pursuit of an eternal moment, like angels without wings. In their wake they leave broken hearts and broken dreams. But they persist, because they believe they are pursuing a higher order.

I hope you can avoid becoming one of these men. It is not easy. The first brush with your sexuality will overwhelm you with its power, and it is only natural to become awestruck in the face of that power.

But I want you to remember an old adage. It says that we humans are destined to live with our feet on the earth and our heads in the heavens, and we can never be at peace because we are pulled both ways.

Nowhere is the truth more clearly revealed than in our sexuality. It sits right in the middle of our being, pulling us in both directions. If we move our sexuality into the earth and want to glory only in the physical, we are no better than the other animals, and soon our lives seem empty and unfulfilled. If we try to remove our sexuality from the sensations of our bodies and turn it into a disembodied celebration of the spiritual, we are doomed to come crashing back to earth each time we try to take wing.

We are neither animals nor angels. We are something else — we are humans — part spiritual and part physical, and those two parts are combined into one: A true sexuality acknowledges both these dimensions and tries to embrace them both in the act of love.

You need to accept this in yourself. Having sex is what the animals do. Achieving mystical union is what the angels do. We alone can make love, where the physical and the spiritual commingle in a single, joyous act.

Know this act, celebrate this act. But, most of all, honor this act. When you share love with a woman, you share one of the greatest mysteries of human existence. Don't demean yourself and her by using it to chase some personal intoxication.

It is only by being totally present to each other, both physically and spiritually, that the true mystery reveals itself.

CHAPTER 24

Making Love

I AM NOT GOING TO GIVE YOU A HOW-TO MANUAL on making love. You will find your way well enough on your own. Besides, there aren't enough pages in all the books in the world to explain the act of making love, partly because it will always remain a mystery beyond our understanding, and partly because it is different for each person, with each person, and between every set of partners.

This is something young people often fail to understand. They look for "good" lovers; they try to turn themselves into "great lovers" by mastering techniques and positions found in books. They airily assess their performances and rate their partners. They blame unsatisfactory sexual experiences on their partners, claiming that he or she was a "lousy lover."

They completely miss the key fact that the sexual act is not one experience. It is different with every person and for every person. It is a miraculous experience that takes place between people, not within two separate individuals.

With one woman you may find yourself ripping and tearing at each other in an animal passion. With another, you may find yourself gently caressing each other into a blissful ecstasy that approaches spiritual union. With yet another you may feel distance, even revulsion, and find your mind a million miles away. And with another, you may find a friendly sharing that is surrounded with warmth but devoid of any capacity to transport you into another realm.

You may discover that you are a great lover with one woman and a horrible lover with another. A woman you thought was a poor lover may turn out to be the most wonderful lover another man ever had. You can never know, until you actually share your bodies, what is going to be revealed in the act of love, because it is in the experience created by the two of you that the truth is revealed.

This mysterious revelation is the source of much sexual confusion and heartbreak, as well as much sexual joy. Like it or not, there is such a thing as sexual chemistry. There are lovers who have nothing in common in the daily affairs of life, but their sexual chemistry is so strong and compelling that they cannot free themselves from its grip. There are people who love each other to the depths of their souls but cannot find themselves in unison sexually. Their most heartfelt efforts to share each other physically end up as clumsy gropings that always seem to be studied and wooden. Try as they might, they are always out of rhythm, out of time.

This does not mean that either of them is a bad lover. It just means that the chemistry somehow is wrong, and despite their best intentions, nothing they can do will right it.

Most lovers eventually fall somewhere in between. They are not continuously swept into a state of ecstatic obliteration with their partners, and they are not eternally held down by a fumbling clumsiness. They make their way together, sometimes in unison, sometimes in mutual isolation, struggling and sharing and feeling the ebbs and flows of their own and their partner's passion. They may not always feel the delirious ecstasy of total sexual annihilation, but they do know the incomparable intimacy of two individuals who care for each other above all others, and for a moment in time are closer to each other than to anyone else. They see each other in a way that only lovers ever see each other, and know each other with a knowledge that is deeper than thought and intellect. This may not be annihilation into mystical ecstasy, but it is enough.

The key is to recognize that this warm glow of intimacy is where a good sexual relationship ends up. You may begin in ecstasy. You may always have moments of almost spiritual transport. But in every relationship, passion cools. It is the inevitable result of familiarity. Over time, the absolute, insatiable hunger that begins any sexual encounter loses some of its savor. A veneer of familiarity and routine begins to form over your sexual experience, and the ability to lose yourself totally in the act begins to lessen.

You can run from this seeming loss of intensity and seek other partners who can provide you with the intensity that comes with novelty. Or you can push the limits of your sexual activities even further into the bizarre in an attempt to keep the intensity alive. But these efforts are as doomed as any others. Your sexual experience passes through stages, just like all of life, and the cooling of sexual passion is part of that passage.

Nonetheless, you will find some lovers more exciting than others. Some of the most exciting may not even be partners toward whom you feel any great depth of human love. But relationships in which the only real commonality is shared physical ecstasy eventually come to a sorry end as passion subsides and the true lack of commitment to the wholeness of the other person begins to show.

If you and your partner love each other deeply, your love will grow up around the physical passion and will fill the space where total passion begins to cool. You will soon blend your love for each other, knowledge of each other, honest desire for each other's happiness, and shared life experiences into a sexual expression that makes up in intimacy for anything that it lacks in passionate intensity. Intimacy eventually overtakes intensity as the true reward and human satisfaction of being lovers, and your hunger for each other will reach a new and deeper level.

As a man, your job is to work toward this intimacy with your partner. This means looking to her sexual needs before your own. If she is sexually passive, meet her with gentleness. If she wants to lead and control sexually, respect that desire. If she is a frightened lover, try to calm that fright. If she is wild and biting and scratching, meet her abandonment with your own.

Reach out to her, find the ways and rhythms of her sexual nature, and let her express herself and fulfill herself through your shared act of love. Do not try to inflict your love on her. Build an intimacy based on total sharing and trust, and let her love take wing in the way that is most natural to her. Celebrate her sexual uniqueness and build upon it to create the unique beauty of the two of you together.

If this sounds too passive — as if you are giving up too much of your own sexual needs — let me assure you that it is not. We men are a much simpler sexual mechanism than are women. Once we get an erection, the deed is effectively over; it is just a matter of time and friction.

For a woman it is more complicated. We are entering her; she is opening herself to us. There is a greater quality of assent involved. As a result, there is more complexity and nuance in her sexual response. It is not enough that we are there physically; she needs to feel that we are there emotionally.

A man who pays heed only to his own simple sexual response is there only physically. He is not being a man in the best sense of the word, even if he thinks he is performing admirably. The most he can hope to be is a sexual athlete. He can never hope to be a true lover unless he looks past his own simple sexual mechanism and makes himself totally present to the emotional and physical needs of his lover. He needs to realize that making love is an act of giving, and the greatest gift he can give is to make a woman secure in her own love.

This sometimes means going against the instincts of our own bodies. It is no great revelation that men and women have different sexual trajectories. We men rise sharply in a surge of passion, and when the moment of release comes, it is as if someone turned on the lights and we are thrown, disoriented, back into the ordinary. Women rise more slowly, in an oceanic crescendo that reaches a peak of passion, then cools.

They want to feel our presence as they rise, and after they

reach their peak, they want to be "loved down," not dropped from their sexual heights. They don't understand the sense of shock we experience upon release, and they are hurt by men who turn from them abruptly, even though that abruptness is just a reflection of our rapid descent back to the ordinary. They want to feel that we loved them, not that we loved the act. So it is important that we override our sexual instincts and reach out from our disorientation to show them the love we feel in our hearts, even if the feeling has momentarily left our bodies.

This is the kind of giving by which a true lover is measured. If you do not put the satisfaction of your partner — both physical and emotional — at the heart of your sexual experience, you will always be deficient as a lover. You may be a great lover in your own mind, and you may even be able to drive some women to a brink of physical frenzy. But the ultimate magic of making love, when two people come together to make something new and shared, will always elude you. There will be a subtle shadow between the two of you that says, "I am here for my own needs," and it will not go away.

Remember, your sexuality cannot lie. If you are just exploring the richness of women, it will show. If you are just building your own ego by unleashing the physical passion in women, it will show. Whatever your true motivation, it will show, even if you don't recognize it yourself. And your lovers will know. They may not say it, but they will feel it.

This is the magical knowledge that lovemaking reveals. It tells the truth of the heart. You can try to hide that truth, but soon the lie grows large.

I don't want you to live that lie. I want you to know the truth of two people so close and caring that there seems to be no distance. I want you to know the joy of tears rolling down your cheeks from the beauty you have shared. But most of all, I want you to be able to look in the eyes of the woman in your arms and say, "I love you," with a pure heart.

If you can, you are truly making love. If you can't, you are just having sex. And the distance between the two is the distance between the earth and the heavens.

CHAPTER 25

The Haunted Heart

HERE IS A STORY THAT MOST MEN KNOW, but few men will tell. It is the story about the ghosts of past lovers, and how they haunt your heart.

The story begins in adolescence, when a boy carries with him a fantasy about the perfect lover. She is shrouded in mystery and beauty — not at all a real women with hopes and fears and the daily cares of life. In fact, she contains few details at all. She is an evocation, a dream, a perfume to the spirit.

This woman of mystery lives somewhere deep in his fantasy, until one day he believes he has found her — the woman of his dreams. She is everything he ever wanted. He pursues her, she responds, and he is alive like never before. Every waking moment is spent dreaming of her. Every moment away from her is agony. When he is with her he looks into her eyes and wants to cry with joy at the incredible good fortune that has brought this beauty into his life.

He wants to touch her. Eventually he does. His body aches for her. He wants to give himself to her, to take her, to know her, to love her.

They struggle with the decision, spending long nights of agonized discussion and desperate gropings. Finally they make love.

They lose themselves for hours, days. They are adrift on a sea of pure, heedless passion. Slowly, this passion cools. They begin to spend their ordinary hours together.

She becomes more of a person and less of a dream. She has needs. She gets angry and has habits. He irritates her; she irritates him. Their sexual hunger falls out of balance. He finds his mind drifting, or he feels her turning inward even as her body pretends to be one with his.

Out of the corner of his eye he begins to notice other women. They seem more attractive. Their laugh has more song in it. They are closer to the dream.

The woman he once thought would fill his life seems empty and ordinary.

Soon there is nothing left but lovemaking. Their passion is hollow. They are together in body but absent in spirit. There are tears and fights and long goodbyes. There are promises that "maybe someday," and gentle claims that "if it is meant to be, it will be."

Eventually they part. Their hearts are wounded and their emotions rage. Sadness smothers the one who was left. Guilt, relief, anger, and self-hatred swirl around the one who did the leaving.

Time passes. The wounds are less.

Another woman comes along. The dance begins again.

Soon they are in each other's arms. It is both harder and easier this time. He looks into her eyes. She is beautiful. But far down, where only the heart can see, is another image.

It is the woman he first loved, the woman who came before.

He loses himself in passion. They become one in that magical way that is the gift of lovemaking. But the image is not gone. It haunts like an echo.

She is there: the ghost of the past lover.

The dance continues. Woman after woman after woman, each one different, each one like a new springtime. He finds parts of himself he never knew existed. He feels love in ways his heart and body never imagined.

But every time, he hears the echoes. No matter how he gives himself, no matter how strong his love, his bed is filled with ghosts of former lovers. And with each woman, there are more ghosts.

He cannot say it, even to himself, but his heart is less than it was. The wounds have turned to scars and the joys of past passions have taken root in the hidden corners of his memory. His love, no matter how pure, is filled with echoes.

He begins to understand a truth, at once terrible and beautiful. He begins to see that the women he has loved are not memories, they are presences. Making love to them has made them alive in his heart forever. He begins to realize that all of those lovers — the one-night stands, the deep yearning passions — were little marriages, eternal unions, each establishing a claim that cannot be denied.

He knows that there has been a price for the love he has given. His love is no longer pure. The memory of every lover shares his bed, and will forever more.

And so, be careful with your love. Do not give it casually. Take the risks you must to find the love you must. But remember that each love is a marriage and each will be part of you forever. Each decreases, by the smallest amount, your capacity to give yourself totally to another, because each one fills a small space in your heart that can never be occupied by another.

Choose carefully and tenderly. Touch has a memory of its own.

CHAPTER 26

Partners and Marriage

I HAVE NEVER MET A MAN who didn't want to be loved. But I have seldom met a man who didn't fear marriage. Something about the closure seems constricting, not enabling. Marriage seems easier to understand for what it cuts out of our lives than for what it makes possible within our lives.

When I was younger this fear immobilized me. I did not want to make a mistake. I saw my friends get married for reasons of social acceptability, or sexual fever, or just because they thought it was the logical thing to do. Then I watched as they and their partners became embittered and petty in their dealings with each other. I looked at older couples and saw, at best, mutual toleration of each other. I imagined a lifetime of loveless nights and bickering days and could not imagine subjecting myself or someone else to such a fate.

And yet, on rare occasions, I would see old couples who somehow seemed to glow in each other's presence. They seemed really in love, not just dependent upon each other and tolerant of each other's foibles. It was an astounding sight, and it seemed impossible. How, I asked myself, can they have survived so many years of sameness, so much irritation at the other's habits? What keeps love alive in them, when most of us seem unable to even stay together, much less love each other?

The central secret seems to be in choosing well. There is something to the claim of fundamental compatibility. Good people can create a bad relationship, even though they both dearly want the relationship to succeed. It is important to find someone with whom you can create a good friendship from the outset.

Unfortunately, it is hard to see clearly in the early stages. Sexual hunger draws you to each other and colors the way you see yourselves together. It blinds you to the thousands of little things by which relationships eventually survive or fail.

You need to find a way to see beyond this initial, overwhelming sexual fascination.

Some people choose to involve themselves sexually and ride out the most heated period of sexual attraction in order to see what is on the other side. This can work, but it can also leave a trail of wounded hearts.

Others deny the sexual altogether in an attempt to get to know each other apart from the sexuality. But they cannot see clearly, because the presence of unfilled sexual desire looms so large that it keeps them from having any normal perception of what life would be like together.

The truly lucky people are the ones who manage to become longtime friends before they realize they are attracted to each other. They get to know each other's laughs, passions, sadnesses, and fears. They see each other at their worst and at their best. They share time together before they get swept up into the entangling intimacy of their sexuality.

This is ideal but not often possible. If you fall under the spell of your sexual attraction immediately, you need to look beyond it for other keys to compatibility.

One of these is laugher. Laughter tells you how much you will enjoy each other's company over the long term. If your laughter together is good and healthy, and not at the expense of others, then you have a healthy relationship to the world. Laughter is the child of surprise. If you can make each other laugh, you can always surprise each other. And if you can always surprise each other, you can always keep the world around you new.

Beware of a relationship in which there is no laughter. Even the most intimate relationships based only on serious-ness have a tendency to turn dour. Over time, sharing a com-mon serious viewpoint on the world tends to turn you against those who do not share the same viewpoint, and your relationship can become based on being critical together.

After laughter, look for a partner who deals with the world in a way you respect. When two people first get together, they tend to see their relationship as existing only in the space between the two of them. They find each other endlessly fascinating, and the overwhelming power of the emotions they are sharing obscures the outside world. As the relationship ages and grows, the outside world becomes important again. If your partner treats people or circum-stances in a way you can't accept, you will inevitably come to grief. Look at the way she cares for others and deals with the daily affairs of life. If that makes you love her more, your love will grow. If it does not, be careful. If you do not respect the way you each deal with the world around you, eventually the two of you will not respect each other.

Look also at how your partner confronts the mysteries of life. We live on the cusp of poetry and practicality, and the real life of the heart resides with the poetic. If one of you is deeply affected by the mystery of the unseen in life and relationships, while the other is drawn only to the literal and practical, you must take care that the distance does not become an unbridgeable gap that leaves you each feeling isolated and misunderstood.

There are many other keys, but you must find them for yourself. We all have unchangeable parts of our hearts that we will not betray and private commitments to a vision of life that we will not deny. If you fall in love with someone who cannot nourish those inviolable parts of you, or if you cannot nourish them in her, you will find yourselves growing further apart until you live in separate worlds where you share the business of life, but never touch each other where the heart lives and dreams. From there it is only a small leap to the cataloging of petty hurts and daily failures that leaves so many couples bitter and unsatisfied with their mates.

So choose carefully and well. If you do, you will have chosen a partner with whom you can grow, and then the real miracle of marriage can take place in your life.

I pick my word carefully when I speak of miracle. But I think it is not too strong a word. There is a miracle in marriage. It is called transformation.

Transformation is one of the most common events of nature. The seed becomes the flower. The cocoon becomes the butterfly. Winter becomes spring and love becomes a child.

We never question these, because we see them around us every day. To us they are not miracles, though if we did not know them they would be impossible to believe.

Marriage is a transformation we choose to make. Our love is planted like a seed, and in time it begins to flower. We cannot know the flower that will bloom, but we can be sure that a bloom will come. If you have chosen carefully and wisely, the bloom will be good. If you have chosen poorly or for the wrong reason, the bloom will be flawed.

We are quite willing to accept the reality of negative transformation in marriage. It was negative transformation that always terrified me about the bitter marriages I feared when I was younger. It never occurred to me to question the dark miracle that transformed love into harshness and bitterness. Yet I was unable to accept the possibility that the first heat of love could be transformed into something positive that was actually deeper and more meaningful than the heat of fresh passion. All I could believe in was the power of this passion and the fear that when it cooled I would be left with something lesser and bitter.

But there is positive transformation as well. Like negative transformation, it results from a slow accretion of little things. But instead of death by a thousand blows, it is growth by a thousand touches of love. Two histories intermingle. Two separate beings, two separate presences, two separate consciousnesses come together and share a view of the life that passes before them. They remain separate, but they also become one. There is an expansion of awareness, not a closure and a constriction, as I had once feared.

This is not to say that tension and traps don't exist. Tension and traps are part of every choice of life, from celibate to monogamous to having multiple lovers. Each choice contains within it the lingering doubt that the road not taken is somehow more fruitful and exciting, and each becomes dulled to the richness that it alone contains.

But only marriage allows life to deepen and expand and be leavened by the knowledge that two have chosen, against all odds, to become one. Those who live together without marriage can know the pleasure of shared company, but there is a specific gravity in the marriage commitment that deepens that experience into something richer and more complex.

So do not fear marriage, just as you should not rush into it for the wrong reasons. It is an act of faith and it contains within it the power of transformation. If you believe in your heart that you have found someone with whom you are able to grow, if you have sufficient faith that you can resist the endless attraction of the road not taken and the partner not chosen, if you have the strength of heart to embrace the cycles and seasons that your love will experience, then you may be ready to seek the miracle that marriage offers.

If not, then wait. The easy grace of a marriage well made is worth your patience. When the time comes, a thousand flowers will bloom.

CHAPTER 27

Staying Faithful

HOW CAN YOU STAY FAITHFUL to one woman? Every woman is like a different country, with a different smell, a different feel, a different spirit. It seems impossible not to want to explore this richness once you know it is there.

And once you have known more than one woman, you know that each woman brings you alive in a different way. How can you turn your back on this knowledge when each time you love another the world is revealed anew?

It is not easy. The lure is always there.

No matter how much you love your wife, no matter how much you value your partner, another woman is going to come along and bring something alive in you that you thought was dead or never knew existed. She is going to fascinate you and obsess you and fill you with desire. You are going to want her and it is going to feel natural.

What are you to do when this takes place?

Some men follow their instincts. They believe that the power of attraction is natural and there is no reason to deny it. Other men struggle against the fascination and try to resist it.

I am lucky. I have my left leg to remind me. It sometimes is wiser than my heart. Here is what happened:

Several years ago, while walking across a parking lot, I slipped on a patch of ice. My legs went out from under me. As I went down I heard a crack like a rifle shot from my left leg.

At first I didn't think anything was too wrong. The fall had seemed so ordinary and uneventful. For months I didn't even have my leg X-rayed. When I finally did, the doctors found that a bone had snapped in two.

They did what they had to — put me in a cast, put me on crutches, and sent me off to heal. I was lucky, they said. The bone had stayed in alignment. When it healed it would be strong as new, maybe even stronger.

They were half right. The bone is mended. It is as strong as new, maybe even stronger. But it has not healed. It lives like a memory in the back of my mind, and every time I slip or begin to lose my balance that rifle crack cuts through my consciousness and I see, in an instant too small for thought, the entire event taking place again before me.

My leg may be healed, but I am not. I am scarred. No matter how strong the bone might be, my mind is still afraid. It will be afraid forever, and I will never totally trust the ground beneath me again.

Whenever I feel a surge of attraction to a woman, I think of that leg. I think of how I took it for granted and assumed it would always be there. I think about how, in a moment, it snapped, and how for the rest of my life I will always be uncertain about it, unable to trust it no matter how much I tell myself it is stronger and safer than ever.

Being unfaithful snaps a relationship as surely as that fall snapped my bone. At first it may seem like nothing. Over time, you may even be able to mend the break so that the relationship is stronger than ever. But it is not healed. The scar remains, and it will haunt you forever.

Is any affair worth this?

That is something you have to decide.

You may think so, if your heart is dead with your partner and the two of you are locked in a joyless union that neither can end, or if the two of you chose each other at a time when you were too weak or too young or too unaware of who you and she were, or if you have changed, and are pulling each other downward in a spiral of anger and violence you cannot stop.

But what if you are merely being seduced by the lure of the new? What if you are fixated on the sensation that begins every love affair but cools as surely as the seasons turn? What if you are mistaking sexual attraction for love? What if you are really in love with love, and no woman will ever satisfy your fantasy?

Then what will you gain by following the lure of a new lover?

These are questions you have to ask. For every man who spends his nights with a woman in a loveless bed, there is a man who leaves a good and loving relationship to chase a fantasy that will come crashing down around him as soon as the novelty wears off and the stuff of daily life begins to intervene.

Think carefully before you risk the wholeness of the love

you have gained. None of us is immune to the lure of the lilt-
ing laugh or the winsome smile. And none of us is so completely filled by our partners that we cannot be captivated by
someone who calls forth new hopes and distant dreams.

Human hearts and lives are involved, and they are far
more precious than bones. If a single snap of a leg has me
doubting the earth below me, what would the crack of a
heart do to something as fragile as love?

CHAPTER 28

Fatherhood

LITTLE IS PERFECT IN OUR LIVES. We dream of perfect love, we try to become perfect people, we challenge ourselves to see the universe as a perfect creation. But all our efforts and struggles are doomed to disappointment. We are not perfect. We are fraught with self-interest and unquenchable longings. Nothing is ever enough.

But there is one place where perfection is given to us in all its wholeness:

Fatherhood.

When you look upon a child you have made, there are no limitations and longings. You are looking with a perfect love.

This is only natural. A child is born with a perfect love and dependence on its parents. It offers itself fully, unconsciously, in the complete unity of its being. There are no conditions and there are no motives. In its lack of self-consciousness it offers itself as a perfect gift.

In the perfection of its love it calls forth the perfection of yours.

For one shining moment, made flesh in time, you experience that oneness that comes from wanting nothing more, nothing less, than the life you have been given.

I thought I never wanted to be a father. A child seemed to be a series of limitations and responsibilities that offered no reward. But when I experienced the perfection of fatherhood, the rest of the world remade itself before my eyes.

I was not limited; I was freed from the fear of limitations. I was not saddled with responsibilities; responsibilities ceased to be a burden.

Nature aligned itself. My fatherhood made me understand my parents and to honor them more for the love they gave. My sonhood was revealed to me in its own perfection and I understood the reason the Chinese so value filiality, the responsibility of the son to honor the parents.

I saw my own imperfection cast in high relief, because I knew how much I wanted to do things right. I felt the unity of generations cascading into generations from the beginning of time. I felt something in the world that was more important than I was.

And that was just the beginning. I knew every other man with different eyes. I hated war with a new passion, but knew what I would fight to save. I loved women for the gift they carried within, not only for the beauty they showed without.

I knew a new kind of love that was devoid of self-interest and desire.

In my bondage to a child I had found true freedom.

The power of this experience can never be explained. It is one of those joyful codings that rumbles in the species far below understanding. When experienced, it makes you one with all men in a way that fills you with warmth and harmony.

This is not to say that becoming a father automatically makes you a good father. Fatherhood, like marriage, is a constant struggle against your limitations and self-interests. But the urge to be a perfect father is there, because your child is a perfect gift. In your heart you know perfection, and it sets a standard that lifts you upward in your daily life.

So move cautiously toward fatherhood. It is much easier to become a father than to be one. When you become a father your whole life suddenly becomes measured against your vision of what good fatherhood should be.

And if your life is not in order — if you have not married well, if you are haunted by personal demons that eat away at your life, if you do not have the discipline that fatherhood requires — you will live in a private shame that will drag you downward and keep you from being the father that lives in your heart. Nothing — not alcohol, not other women, not running away — will shield you from the harsh truth of your failure.

So look upon fatherhood as a gift. It is one of life's common miracles, available to everyone and given freely to us all. A child, whether healthy or ill, misshapen or beautiful, opens the world into a new sunlight. It is an experience greater than a dream.

If it is true that God loves us like a father, we can all rest peacefully. We are loved with a perfect love.

CHAPTER 29

The Burden of Age

YOUR HEART IS REVEALED in the way you treat the elders. Like children, the elders are sometimes a burden. But unlike children, they offer no hope or promise. They are a weight and an encumbrance and a mirror of our own mortality. It takes a person of great heart to see past this fact and to see the wisdom elders have to offer, and to serve them out of gratitude for the life they have passed on to us.

I hope that you will be such a person.

It is not easy in this culture. We have lost a feel for our elders. They are a sad, gray presence, hidden behind clumsy phrases like "elderly," "senior citizens," "retired persons." They are tolerated out of guilt, feared for the burden they represent, or shunted aside into irrelevance. They are not loved and honored and sought out for the wisdom that their years have given them.

Chances are you will find yourself of two minds about elders. Some will be fascinating to you, especially the ones who seem to carry their youth with them into old age. Others will be frightening to you for their ugliness or their nearness to death. Still others will bring you great pleasure because they want so much to please you and demand so little of you. But no matter how they make you feel, you should always watch them carefully. They were you and you will be them. You carry the seeds of your old age in you at this very moment, and they hear the echoes of their childhood each time they see you.

You will find that many old people are not pleasant. They are as filled with themselves and their own concerns as the very young are. They ask you to think about them and their feelings with little or no concern for yours.

When you meet such elders you must not take them in the wrong way. Like young children, old people are dependent on the world around them and they very often fear their own loss of importance. They face the uncertainty of death and are often embittered that the world they worked so hard to create is being discarded by the generations now in power. Their bodies are giving out on them. They increasingly find themselves surrounded only by people their own age, because they know that the young would rather be apart from them. They often live in memories.

When you meet such elders you must not be blinded by their unpleasantness. When you are tired, or ill, or full of anger and pain, you, too, may not be pleasant. For many elders, these are the conditions of their lives. But beneath the surface of their actions is a wisdom you can gain nowhere else.

Even if theirs was the simplest, most limited, most ordinary of lives, they saw the world into which you have come. No other past generation is as close to yours; no other life so near in time. Their stories have the blood of your life running through them. You will never be so close to the world that gave birth to you as you are when speaking to them. For that and that alone you should honor and revere them and give them your ear. You are bonded in time.

It is important that you avoid the pitfall of pity when dealing with elders. Too many people, under the guise of caring, patronize and demean the very old by treating them like children. They speak to them loudly, or as if they were simpletons. They interpret the elder's concern for the minutiae of life as a return to the infantile. In actions and in manner they strip the elders of the very respect they claim to be giving them.

These people are, in their own way, causing as much harm as those who ignore the elders. They are, through their actions, holding up mirrors in which the elders must see their infirmity, not mirrors in which they can see their humanity. True caring and respect serve the weakness, but mirror only the human and the strength. Caring and respect listen, laugh, and even challenge. They assume that the words and actions of the elders are to be taken seriously.

You must remember that, even in their infirmity, elders seek and value their dignity. They want, above all else, to feel that their lives are valued, and that their time on earth has not been wasted. If you can go to them with a pure heart, unblinded by notions of false reverence and unaffected by self-serving feelings of pity, if you can value them and allow them to share the fruits of their experience, however simple those fruits might be, you will be performing the greatest act a heart can perform.

You will be loving them, not serving them.

CHAPTER 30

The Gift of Age

L AST WEEK I HELPED BURY Dan Needham. Dan was ninety-five when he died, the oldest living hereditary chief of the Red Lake Ojibwe. I got to know him several years ago when I was working on an oral history project.

I would bring young people to his home to talk with him. They would sit patiently in his living room, listening to him tell stories about his grandfather's battles with the Sioux, and reminisce about the lives the Indian people had led during the lean years of the Great Depression.

The young people were not always attentive, but Dan didn't mind. He knew it was important for them to hear about the past, and he was confident that their hearts were listening, even if their ears weren't.

Dan always made us feel welcome. He was always dressed and waiting at the door when we came, and he never asked us to leave early, even though I could see the exhaustion in his face. He answered the young people's questions as best he could, straining to hear their words and trying to keep himself from drifting off into his own reveries. Sometimes he would repeat himself or go on too long about a subject, and the students would nudge each other or roll their eyes. He saw their glances but never let on. He bore the burdens and insights of age with a gentle good humor.

In the last several years Dan deteriorated physically. He moved to a nursing home and seldom got out of bed. But he was always willing to visit, and always gracious. He accepted the failing of his body, and when it finally could go no further, he gave himself over willingly to the unknown. I have never known anyone who accepted the passing of life with such peace and calm.

When he died, few people noticed. Dan had outlived his generation, and his life was already little more than a memory. But when he died he took more than memories with him. He took the flash of his eyes as he spoke of the time his warrior grandfather was brought back from a battle on a horse-drawn travois. He took the smile that came when he described going for a ride in a Model-T for the first time.

He took the life that animated the stories that now are nothing more than words on a page or tales told to children. He took the sense of presence and grace that had grown so pure and natural in those ninety-five years of life. He took the wisdom of age and the touch of the past. And nothing will ever replace them.

I don't know if the young people who used to visit him realize this loss. I'm not sure that they ever saw anything more than a rambling old man with a bad eye and skin mottled with liver spots. I don't know if they heard his stories or if they even cared. For them, life was in the future. Dan only represented life in the past.

None of them was at his funeral. They had places to go and lives to live. Dan would have said that was just fine. Bury the dead quickly and honorably, and leave life to the living.

But the dead are not so easily buried. Their lives have touched the edges of ours, and have made us who we are. We live in a world made by their hands; we sat in their presence and saw who we will become.

The young people who visited Dan will find this out soon enough. They will keep his stories alive, and he will become one of their stories.

When they show their children a Model-T, they will tell them about the old man who used to ride in one with his friends.

When their children ask about the old days when the treaties were signed, they will tell about the old man whose grandfather was at those treaties and saw the cavalry playing cards while their cannons were pointed at the Ojibwe camp-sites.

As they get older and try to pass their knowledge along, they will understand the wisdom of that old man who just smiled while they whispered and giggled and nudged. And as they approach their death, they will remember the peace and calm with which that old man approached his death, and perhaps it will give them courage.

By the time they are old he will be their friend, far closer than he was when they were sitting at his feet. They will grow into his wisdom and make it their own.

That is the way it is with the elders. When we are young, they seem irrelevant. But each touch we make with them makes us wiser, though we never know it until it is time. The young people who visited Dan are wiser by years than if they had never known him. The ones who watched and listened are wiser still.

Dan Needham is dead, and we have lost a good man. But he lives on, as all the dead live on, etched in our memories and stored in the forgotten corners of our lives. His passing is cause for sadness, but his life is cause for celebration. To those of us who knew him he gave more than knowledge of our past. He gave us wisdom to understand our future.

CHAPTER 31

Death

DEATH IS OUR COMMON MYSTERY. Like birth and love, it is a bond that unites us all. Yet none of us can know for certain what it contains or what it portends.

We have glimpses — from those who have experienced clinical death and returned to tell what they saw, from great religious tracts like *The Tibetan Book of the Dead* and *The Egyptian Book of the Dead*. And we have promises — from all the faiths and religions.

We can never know for certain which, if any, are true. Everyone must meet death alone, so it remains the great private preparation for each of us.

What would I have you know about death?

Once many years ago I was present at a total eclipse of the sun. I had climbed to the top of a high hill and had sat down to wait. It was early morning, slightly past sunup. Birds were singing in the trees around me. Far below on a hillside cows were grazing and horses rustled in the tall grasses.

When the moment came the sun began to darken. The horses were silent, the cows stood still. The birds ceased their chirping. As the sun disappeared behind the moon, the earth became still. The cows sank to their knees and the birds placed their heads beneath their wings.

Only the ghostly corona of the hidden sun remained to cast a fragile light on the enveloping darkness. There was no wind. There was no sound. The light of the sun had been taken from us and the world was cast into a great darkness.

At that moment something momentous happened: I no longer feared death. I felt annihilation, but annihilation into a oneness. I thought of my uncle who at that moment lay dying thousands of miles away. I thought of his fear and his loneliness and wished for all the world that he could have been with me for those seconds when the sun gave up its light.

I can't put a name to the knowledge I gained. It was too far beyond the human for me to understand. But I know it had to do with death, and I know it had to do with the great darkness into which we all must go.

There was a peace there, a peace that surpasses all understanding.

When fears of death overwhelm me, as they do at moments of sickness or great danger, I think of that hilltop and the birds with their heads tucked beneath their wings. All of us — me, the birds, the cows, and the horses — had been taken up into something larger than life itself.

Our selves had been obliterated; our individuality taken from us. Yet there was no impulse to scream against that obliteration. We were subsumed into something so great that we accepted it like the tranquil embrace of a long-sought sleep.

If that moment on the hillside contained truth — and I think it did — we do death no justice by measuring it against ourselves. We are too small; it is too great. What we fear is only the loss of the self, and the self knows eternity like a shadow knows the sun.

So, fear dying if you must. It takes from us the only life that we can understand, and that is a worthy loss to mourn. But do not fear death. It is something too great to celebrate, too great to fear. Either it brings us to a judgment, so it is ours to control by the kind of life we live, or it annihilates us into the great rhythm of nature, and we join the eternal peace of the revolving heavens.

In either case, I believe in my heart that it is ours to trust.

In the brief moment when I stood on that hillside while the earth's light went out, I felt no indifference and no sense of loss. Instead I felt an unutterable sense of gain, a shattering of all my own boundaries into a vast sense of peace.

If that was a moment of death, death should hold no terror, and we should embrace our dying as a momentary passage into the great harmony of eternity.

Perhaps we cannot hear that harmony now. Perhaps we even hear it as a vast and empty silence. But we should not be deceived. That vastness is not empty, it is a presence. Even in the greatest places the silence has a sound.

A Father's Reflection

THE SUN HANGS HEAVY in the breathless August sky as I bring this book to a close. It is deep summer now — a time of resting, a time of completions, a time when the shadows are long upon the land.

I used to dread these waning days of August. They seemed suspended in time. Summer had given up its promise and the dark whisperings of winter rode upon the edges of the wind.

Now I love these days. There is wisdom in their stillness. In the fields the promise of spring has found its voice. Yet the light has thinned and the animals have distance in their eyes.

It is a good time to end.

It is my time, too, this midlife of the seasons. Like the earth itself, I stand watchful over the changing landscape of my life.

From here I can see the springtime promise of you who are coming up behind me. I can feel the surging of your hopes and the sharp, fresh edges of your dreams. But I can also sense the coming knowledge of age with its colder cares and darker echoes.

For this brief moment I am one with the generations, a father to my son, a son to my father.

It is a good place to be, and it has changed me.

I am more patient now. Like the crops in the field, I know that there are times to act and times to wait. The seeds I have planted will blossom only when they will, and nothing I can do will rush them.

I am clearer. My youthful desires and dreams have settled into simpler truths, and common kindness often seems enough.

I bear burdens more gladly. The joyous weights of family and fatherhood have softened my heart, and I more willingly embrace the obstacles and limitations of life.

And I know more of love, because I have had it come and go in my life and I treat it with more respect.

But most of all, I am gentler with myself and others, because I know something now of grace — how much our lives are the product of a touch, a glance, a letter never sent or received.

Had I not been on that one certain corner at that one certain moment; had that one hand not reached out to mine when another held back; had I had courage when I stopped in fear, or fear when I went on in courage; had I said "no" when I said "yes"; had I had a dollar more or less, or been born a mile or two nearer to the dawn, my life would have been another, as distant from this life as from a story or a dream.

And so I am thankful. The chances I have received seem more like gifts and less like my due. But for a chance rain or a day of sun, I, too, could have been barren soil, producing nothing, empty of love.

Yes, this is a good season, this midlife. There is peace here, far more than in my youth.

You will learn this peace in your own time. But for now, yours is the season of fresh passions. Embrace it. Celebrate it. Give yourself to its joys and sorrows. But remember to be gentle with yourself and others. We all are children of chance, and none can say why some fields will blossom while others lay brown beneath the August sun.

Care for those around you. Look past your differences. Their dreams are no less than yours, their choices in life no more easily made.

And give. Give in any way you can, of whatever you possess. To give is to love. To withhold is to wither. Care less for your harvest than for how it is shared, and your life will have meaning and your heart will have peace.

Outside, a breeze has risen now. The birches dance and the flowers turn their faces from the wind.

In the distance a loon raises a lonely, haunting call.

It is good to be alive, my son.

It is good to be alive.

ABOUT THE AUTHOR

KENT NERBURN holds a Ph.D. in Religion and Art. He is an internationally recognized artist with sculptures in such settings as Westminster Benedictine Abbey in Mission, British Columbia, and the Peace Museum in Hiroshima, Japan. For several years he worked with the Ojibwe of northern Minnesota helping collect the memories of their tribal elders.

He is the author of *Neither Wolf nor Dog: On Forgotten Roads with an Indian Elder, A Haunting Reverence, Small Graces, Simple Truths,* and *Make Me an Instrument of Your Peace.* He has has also edited three books of Native American writing: *Native American Wisdom, The Wisdom of the Great Chiefs,* and *The Soul of an Indian.*

He lives with his wife, Louise Mengelkoch, and their son, Nicholas, in northern Minnesota.

If you enjoyed *Letters to My Son,* we recommend the following books by Kent Nerburn:

Neither Wolf nor Dog: On Forgotten Roads with an Indian Elder. This winner of the 1995 Minnesota Book Award draws us deep into the world of a Lakota Elder identified only as Dan. With humor, pathos, and insight, we are taken through the myths and stereotypes to the heart of the Native American experience. An unlikely cross between Jack Kerouac and *Black Elk Speaks.*

A Haunting Reverence: Meditations on a Northern Land. In what Robert Bly calls "a rare and honest work," Kent Nerburn writes a powerful exploration of northern Minnesota's natural landscape. Nerburn beautifully merges the incandescent radiance of Native American thought with the intellectual passion of Western sensibilities.

Small Graces: The Quiet Gifts of Everyday Life. A journey through the sacred moments that illuminate our everyday lives. In twenty elegant short pieces, Kent Nerburn celebrates the daily rituals that reveal our deeper truths. *"I believe it will become a classic."* — Dan Millman

New World Library is dedicated to publishing books
and cassettes that inspire and challenge us to improve the
quality of our lives and our world. Our books and cassettes
are available at bookstores everywhere.
For a complete catalog, contact:

New World Library
14 Pamaron Way
Novato, California 94949

Phone: (415) 884-2100
Fax: (415) 884-2199

Or call toll free: (800) 972-6657
Catalog requests: Ext. 50
Ordering: Ext. 52

E-mail: escort@nwlib.com
http://www.nwlib.com